Wry Stories
on
THE ROAD
HOLE

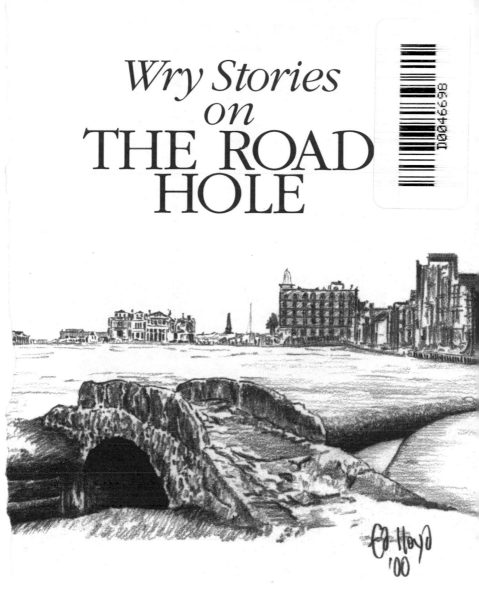

SIDNEY L. MATTHEW

Sleeping Bear Press
PUBLISHER OF FINE BOOKS

St. Andrew

*The X-shaped cross was chosen by Andrew because
he felt unworthy to die on the same type of cross
on which Christ had suffered and died.*

Sketches by Ed Lloyd (c) MM Sidney L. Matthew

(c) MM Sidney L. Matthew

Sleeping Bear Press
310 North Main Street
Chelsea, MI 48118

Printed in USA

10-9-8-7-6-5-4-3-2-1
Library of Congress CIP Data on File
ISBN 1-58536-017-1

For my Friends in St. Andrews, Scotland –
"Lang may yer lums reek"

THE ROAD HOLE

There are a few holes in golf that, having been played only once, are forever engraved in a player's mind. The Road Hole is one of them.

Golf has been played on the area of land which now forms the Old Course at St. Andrews for more than half of the last millennium and many of the features which make the course so unique are those that nature decreed should be there.

The Road Hole however, is a perfect blend of nature and the deviousness of man, combining to present a challenge that, whatever the conditions, is always going to test the skill and nerve of those who play it. Coming so late in the round means one is conscious that, however good the start and middle part of the round may have been, all can come undone at the 17th. The safer you try to play it, the harder it can become.

Possibly more so than any other hole in golf, it offers the opportunity for a seemingly impossible deficit to be recovered, which means, of course, it can also lead to the loss of an almost impregnable lead.

During the Millennium Open, no doubt there will be more tales of disaster, but it is certain that as the Championship concludes, the thoughts of spectators, television viewers, golf writers, and most of all the players in contention, will again be focused on this unique hole, as has been the case since the first St. Andrews Open in 1873.

MICHAEL BONALLACK
CAPTAIN
ROYAL & ANCIENT GOLF CLUB

ACKNOWLEDGMENTS

The notion of compiling a collection of wry stories on the Road Hole was spawned over a wee dram in February 1999, waiting for the snow to melt on the Old Course. The conversation coursed over many banks and braes, and disappeared into the haar. Your author set about researching the background over the succeeding year with the invaluable assistance and contributions of the following kindhearted souls, whose contributions are gratefully acknowledged: Arthur Montford, Charlie Yates, Bill Hyndman, Ronnie Alexander, Robin Waddell, Sir Sean Connery, Sir Michael Bonallack, A.C. "Sandy" Rutherford, Bill Campbell, Vinny Giles, John Fischer III, Rand Jarris, U.S.G.A. Library & Buzz Taylor, R&A Golf Club of St. Andrews, Cilla Jackson, Richard Batchelor, Clark MacKenzie, Mort Olman, John Olman, Malcolm Campbell, Gordon Christie, Iain MacFarlane Lowe, Ian Findlay, F.R. Bobby Furber, St. Andrews University Library Special Collections, Errie Ball, Jimmy Gabrielson, Bill Bridges, Mark Black, Archie Baird, Rick MacKenzie, Bob Henderson, David Joy, Cliff Campbell, and Eldon Steeves.

Grateful acknowledgment is made to the following publishing companies and authors for permission to reprint various short excerpts, sentences, and quotations: *The St. Andrews of Jo Grimond* by Jo Grimond; *The Story of the R&A* by J.B. Salmond; *Challenges & Champions* by John Behrend & Peter N. Lewis; *St. Andrews Town & Gown, Royal & Ancient* by Douglas Young; *St. Andrews Home of Golf* by James K. Robertson; *The Spirit of St. Andrews* by Alister MacKenzie; *Golf Is My Game* by Robert Tyre Jones, Jr.; *Sixty Years of Golf* by Robert Harris; *A Game of Golf* by Francis Ouimet; *The Scottish Golf Book* by Malcolm Campbell; *A History of Golf* by Robert Browning; *Scotland's Gift Golf* by Charles Blair Macdonald.

Thanks also to Sleeping Bear Press and Brian Lewis for producing another enjoyable title, at least from the author's viewpoint, and to Lynne Johnson, who is Sleeping Bear's Sleeping Giant, and has shepherded many of the author's scribblings through the publication assembly line with grace and dignity.

Last, and perhaps foremost, it has been the author's great privilege to meet and work with the internationally known artist Ed Lloyd. When he is not working on his doctorate or teaching the fine art of engineering to worthy students, Ed moonlights, as a professor of pencil drawing as a master art form. There is good reason why Ed's skills are in great demand. His work has graced the pages and enhanced several

other titles by the author, including *Champions of East Lake: Bobby Jones & Friends* (1999) and *Bobby Jones Golf Tips* (1999). His work has been widely exhibited, with portraits on the jazz artists and the Old South. Ed's work on Bobby Jones and Golf is on permanent display at the Georgia Sports Hall of Fame in Macon, Georgia. The author never ceases to marvel at his uncommon genius. While my wife, Linda, knows that I love her, she is also resigned to the fact that the law is a jealous mistress, and that writing these books has required the author to chain himself to his library chair. She should rejoice that there is hope yet for a speedy release, and return to the routine rigors of the welcomed daily routine. My kids (Jennifer, Lauren, and Geoffrey) and my grandkids (Skylar, MacKenzie, and Sydney) will someday get a kick out of the content of these scrawlings.

TO GOD BE THE GLORY.

TABLE OF CONTENTS

INTRODUCTION

BY WILLIAM C. CAMPBELL

The Old Course at St. Andrews is, without a doubt, unique—perhaps not the "best" golf course in the world, or the most difficult, but certainly the most memorable because of its distinctive history, surroundings, and course features. Of these, none is more famous than the Road Hole, i.e., the 17th, which, playing much harder than it looks, is a dangerous and intimidating par 4—arguably the most difficult one anywhere. It can be rewarding, but treat it lightly at your peril! A half century has not dimmed my early impressions of this historic golf hole as a make-or-break tester, with little margin for error.

My first encounter with the Road Hole was during the 1950 British Amateur, in which it played a special role in my sixth round match with Joe Carr of Ireland. In a fourth round match with former British and U.S. Champion Willie Turnesa, I came to the 17th 2-up; the dusk was gathering as our match had begun at 6:30 p.m. After a long drive over the railroad shed to mid-fairway, I hit a 7-iron shot to within three feet of the flagstick; so I won the match 3-1, at 9:45 p.m., with street lights on. So far, so good.

The next evening, after squeaking by the defending champion, Max McCready, in the morning, I came to the Road Hole "all square" with Joe Carr. My drive was similar to the one against Turnesa—through a cold crosswind still from the east, off the North Sea—but this time I chose a 5-iron and hit it a bit too well. The ball landed next to the flagstick, but rolled just through the green and down onto the road. Meanwhile Joe had played his second shot short-right, in proper position for a run-up and putt. My first attempt from the road hung up on the ragged slope and fell back to the road; my next try was better, bouncing up the steep slope to finish five feet short of the cup. Joe missed his 4, so I had the five-footer to halve the hole and remain all square going to 18. As I was about to putt, a church clock tolled the hour of 6:00, so I stepped back and nervously shared the crowd's laughter.

One month earlier, in the final of the North and South Amateur at Pinehurst, Wynsol Spencer and I were "all square" on #17 (the 35th hole of the match) where I had a five-foot putt to stay even with him. Just as I was about to putt, the Community Chapel's clock tolled the hour of 6:00. I stepped back to share the crowd's laughter, and then made the putt, and went on to win on the 37th.

Now, one month later, on the Road Hole, with the cold air blowing under the bill

of my cap and blurring my vision, the tolled hour sent a tingle down my spine and I felt sudden confidence despite the fuzzy cup, and in the ball went. Things were going my way after all. Two holes later, in my fourth extra hole match of that British Amateur, the spell was broken as I lost to Joe Carr's birdie -3 and was suddenly "out" and 3,500 miles from home.

Twenty-one years later, during a practice round before the 1971 Walker Cup Matches, I was approached on the 17th fairway by a stranger who asked me why, in the 1950 Amateur, from the same distance and with a similar wind, I had used a 5-iron vs. Carr instead of the 7-iron vs. Turnesa—a fatal difference (as it turned out) that he had noticed so long ago! My reaction was to ask the stranger's name—one Peter Smith, a senior mathematics master from nearby Anstruther, whom I have enjoyed as a wise and good friend ever since. His unusual question, reflecting detailed memory of championship golf on the Old Course, foretold his encyclopedic knowledge of golf, no less. (Incidentally, in similar conditions in recent years, I have, at best, needed at least a long-iron to reach the 17th green.)

The Road Hole has also been crucial in international team play, thanks to some great approach shots by notable amateurs, such as a superb 4-iron by Jay Haas on the first day of the 1975 Walker Cup Matches, which won the hole and match; another classic 4-iron by Bill Hyndman in the first World Team Championship for the Eisenhower Trophy in October 1958, played under heavy pressure that included the scrutiny of his revered team captain, Bob Jones; and to turn the tables on Hyndman, a picture-perfect 3-iron by Dr. David Marsh in their singles match during the 1971 Walker Cup, that he won by one hole (David has deservedly dined out on that shot ever since).

In that 1971 match, only a few minutes earlier, U.S. player Jim Gabrielsen had two close calls go against him on the Road Hole. The first was his second shot, which looked perfect as it rolled onto the green just to the right of the Road Hole Bunker. The ball hovered at the top of the slope before falling back to the left into the bunker, from which Jim then extricated himself admirably, with his ball landing close to the cup, only to skip past and barely to the back of the green, where it hovered and fell onto the road. Jimmy lost to George McGregor, one down.

So, the Road Hole was critical in Great Britain and Ireland's come-from-behind (13-11) victory in that pivotal Walker Cup match of 1971. It was the 50th anniversary of the first "informal" match and only the second victory by Great Britain and

Ireland in the storied series—the earlier one having also been played on the Old Course in 1938.

Earlier in that 1971 Walker Cup, in the first singles match on the first day, Michael Bonallack was the victim of a cruel and fortuitous stroke by Vinny Giles, whose bladed recovery shot from the road struck the flagstick a hard blow and dropped two feet straight down into the hole, not having touching the green surface at all.

Back to the 1950 British Amateur and a 6th round match between Frank Stranahan and the late Billy (Dynamite) Goodloe of Valdosta, Georgia. The 1950 *British Golf Monthly* sets the stage for what happened at The Road Hole:

The championship, like all international events, brings men of phenomenal physique to battle for the awards. There were many giants, both English and American, but the most remarkable was William L. Goodloe from Georgia, 5 feet 3 inches who weighs 16 stone. His legs are short but his body resembles a top line heavyweight prizefighter. He hit the ball colossal distances. His first drive in the championship was not many yards short of the Swilken Bern. He took a niblick; the ball landed about a yard from the flag and from the jump went into the hole for a two. This was a championship record. Goodloe was colorful and varied in his rig, a bright splash in the great, gray cathedral city. He wore green trousers, a crimson pullover and a tartan Scottish bonnet.

In contrast to Dynamite, Frank Stranahan was a handsome and famous amateur golfer and heir to the Champion sparkplug fortune. Frank was one of the first golfers ever to train using barbells and weights, and his physique showed it well. Stranahan built a wonderful competitive record and was America's leading post - WWII amateur, winning everything in sight except the U.S. Amateur.

In his match with Goodloe, however, Stranahan found himself in a tough position. Coming to the 16th hole, Dynamite had Frank down by two and Frank was fretting. Dynamite hit his approach into the closest bunker on the 16th green. He was up against the lip and his first and second attempts failed. So he pocketed the ball and conceded 16, but was still 1-up. Dynamite hit a tremendous drive off the 17th Road Hole tee. His short iron almost hit the pin and ran over the road into some scruffy grass adjacent to the wall. Stranahan had played his approach shot short and right of the green in proper position and from which he made a cozy approach for a "cinch four." As Dynamite crossed The Road and began to survey his

options, his caddy set his golf bag down on the ground. At that time, The Road and its environs were played as a hazard. But Dynamite did not know that in Great Britain there was no penalty for grounding a club in a hazard unless the player actually changed the position of the ball. Of course, Dynamite's caddy had not affected the lie of his ball. But Dynamite assumed that he had violated the rule anyway when his caddy grounded his clubs in the hazard. So, without seeking a ruling or consulting Frank, Dynamite mistakenly picked up his ball and conceded the hole. That made their match square and Frank won on 18. Later Frank went on to win against Dick Chapman in the final for his second British Amateur title. Sadly for Dynamite, who would have been a colorful and popular champion, he never returned to St. Andrews.

I trust that these recollections will suggest why I hold the Road Hole in such high regard. A 4 or even a 3 will reward a golfer who plays it "just right"—but woe be to him who takes liberties with it!

THE PENULTIMATE HOLE IN GOLF— THE ROAD HOLE AT ST. ANDREWS

The penultimate hole in all of golf is surely the Road Hole at St. Andrews. The Eden Hole (No. 14) is the darling of the press and gets considerably more attention when championships are contested at the Old Course. After all, one must pass through "Hell" (bunker) to reach the salvation of its green. But there can be little quarrel that the Road Hole is the epitome of the game we call "gowlf." The Road Hole beguiles, confounds, challenges, mystifies, exasperates, intrigues, invigorates, impersonates, confronts, intimidates, teases, annihilates, perturbs, agitates, regurgitates, insomniates, subjugates, and those are simply the inaugural 17 emotions evoked by the hole. Not unlike a siren's song, there is a seductive, if not wicked, attraction to this hole which ensnares the imagination of golfers who are long in the tooth and grizzled in the beard. And that is just the beginning.

There is good reason to be vigilant when assessing the strengths of the Road Hole. Too many golf holes are passive in their nature, and consequently they permit the golfer to get the upper hand if he can. Not so with the Road Hole. The Road Hole, unlike any other, rises up from the mists as a conquering aggressor, or at the least, an equal combatant. The Road Hole somewhat indignantly, but justifiably, takes a page from Churchill and announces at the outset in almost Churchillian tones:

> *I will fight the foreign invader on the tee, fight him in the fairway, fight him in the rough and tall grasses, fight him in Scholar's and Progressing bunkers, fight him in the air and on the ground, fight him in the Road and against the wall, fight him in the Road Bunker, and fight him on the putting green. I will never surrender, ever!*

For, you see, this is not just any ordinary golfing hole. This is not an experience soon to be forgotten. I'll have you know that this is the Road Hole of the Old Course at St. Andrews!

Francis Ouimet

CONTEMPT FROM MR. OUIMET'S CADDIE

By Charlie Yates

If ever there is one hole in golf, the best known is No. 17 on the Old Course at St. Andrews. It was a par 5 for many years, but now is considered a 4. From the tee, the ball played in the conventional way is a dogleg right. However, a longer hitter could cut the corner by driving over a woodshed about 200 yards from the tee.

The hole got its name from a cobblestone road that runs alongside the back of the green. If one gets in there, it takes a lot of good luck to get back on the green. I first played the Old Course in 1938 at the time of the Walker Cup Matches. This was the first loss the American team had ever had, but fortunately, I won my singles match by defeating Jimmy Bruen. The match ended on the Road Hole, thanks to a 10-foot putt I made for a 4.

My next visit to St. Andrews was in 1951, when I had the good fortune of going over with Francis Ouimet when he drove himself in as the first American to be Captain of the R&A. He recalled a happening when he first played the Old Course many years before.

Francis said he drove over the woodshed during a practice round and was right in the middle of the fairway, about 200 yards from the green. His caddie was an elderly Scot with perhaps a nip or two in him to keep warm and who obviously had a bet with another caddie about who would win. Francis approached his ball and said, "Please give me my spoon." The caddie said, "Mr. Ouimet, you will be playing your 2 iron." Francis said, "No, I want my spoon." He hit a beautiful shot but, unfortunately, the ball went over the green and into the road. Francis looked around and saw no sign of his caddie but the golf bag was lying on the ground. He looked over toward the clubhouse and saw his caddie headed for the clubhouse. Francis asked him where he was going and the caddie said, "I am quitting. From now on you will be caddying for yourself."

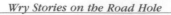

St. Andrews beloved first golf professional, Allan Robertson

WINNING STROKE
WITH A FRYING PAN

The first professional golfer was St. Andrews' favorite son, Allan Robertson. Robertson was a diminutive fellow standing perhaps five feet five inches. But he was lionhearted, and a master at playing with thorn-headed play-clubs and featherie golf balls, which he made in his shop by the links. Allan was also the first man ever to shoot a score below 80 on the Old Course. He returned a score of 79 on September 15, 1858. Allan was never beaten in any stipulated money match from 1840 until his death in 1859. Robertson gave his clubs descriptive names including "The Doctor," "Thraw-Cruik" (wry-neck), and his favorite, called "The Frying Pan." One of the most celebrated strokes made by Allan Robertson was with his Frying Pan at the Road Hole. It was described by Reverend Principal W.W. Tulloch of St. Mary's in his biography, *The Life of Tom Morris*:

Within two holes of the second round Allan and Mr. Wemyss were 1 down and only 2 to play. Campbell of Saddell was in glee. He was backing the likely winners. 'Three five-pound notes to one.' 'Done sir, with you.' The bet was taken by Mr. John Blackwood. Alas! how black for Allan it looked, when, at the 17th hole, Park had put Mr. Hastie on the green, and Mr. Wemyss had put Allan on the road. He had to play 'two more'. 'Fryingpan' [a kind of niblick] in hand, Allan studied the ground and the loft he had to make, the spot where he had to pitch. Back and forwards from ball to hole he went, and then, while Daw, his caddie, whispered in his ear 'Ye can doo't Allan,' he played. The ball was pitched to the top of the footpath, ran down, and trickled into the hole. Great was the applause. His opponents were so much discomfited that Mr. Hastie ran past the hole with his putt, and Park was short. Allan and his partner won the hole.

The Road Hole

ROBBED BY THE ROAD HOLE

The fifth occasion on which St. Andrews hosted the Open Championship was 1885, when Bob Martin won the title for the second time. A legend which has persisted for half a century says that he shouldn't have won at all. Instead, the story has passed down through the ages that St. Andrews professional David Ayton should rightly have won. He was robbed by the Road Hole. The story has been repeatedly published that when Ayton stepped onto the 17th tee on the final round of 36 holes, he held a five-stroke lead. His drive was good enough, and he followed it with a cracking shot with his brassie into the proper position for a run-up stroke to the flagstick. So far, so good. His fortune started to unravel from there. His run-up stroke was much too timid, and the ball was captured by the Devil's Swail, which villainously kidnaps balls that are not hit with conviction and commandeers them to the purgatory of the Road Bunker. Ah well, these things happen. No time to panic. In the twinkle of an eye, the degree of difficulty of Ayton's next shot had increased exponentially from a relatively elementary run-up stoke. Ayton seized his niblick, and one angry man entered the Hellish Pit. It's too bad that Ayton didn't have the benefit of the modern sand wedge. Gene Sarazen did not perfect that helpful implement with plenty of bounce on its sole until 1932. Ayton's club was more akin to a garden tool. The only issue faced by Ayton at that moment was how much force to apply to the stroke. There were only two consequences: damned if you do hit it too hard, and damned if you don't. Ayton erred in the former premise and hit his ball too hard. The ball skittled across the green, and popped up like a jack rabbit onto the Road. Oh well. Not to worry. Concern yes, panic no. He'll just coax the ball onto the green, and go collect the title on the next hole. Careful not to hit it too hard this time. Ayton hit this one too easy. The ball bobbled up onto the bank, and bobbled back down like it was a yo-yo on a string. Ayton now lies five. It's now definitely time to panic. Get the damn ball on the green this time. Uh oh. That was a strong one. Now the ball races over the green and back in the bunker. Now let's review the bidding. Three in the bunker, four on the Road, and lying six back in the bunker. Now time to get one close. Oh, no. Left it in the bunker again. That's seven. Try it again. Nope. That's eight. Take a big blast of sand this time. That's right. Now the ball is out in nine. Now Ayton is tied for the lead with Bob Martin. Except that he needs two more putts to hole out. Unlucky. An 11. That's nine

strokes in 30 yards. As Bernard Darwin would say: "A little old lady with a croquet mallet could have gotten down in eight and won the Open by a stroke." Poor man.

Former R&A historian Bobby Burnett was concerned that the reputation of David Ayton has been unfairly besmirched by hanging this stinking historical albatross around his neck. So Bobby went back to the books to examine the eyewitness accounts and make some sense out of them. Bobby is a careful researcher. He found that none of the contemporary reports on the championship in 1885 said anything about David Ayton engaging in an act of self-destruction on the Road Hole. Indeed, 20 years after the championship in 1906, winner Bob Martin searched his memory for an interview with *Golf Illustrated*. An article published in the April 20, 1906 issue of *Golf Illustrated* quoted Martin as saying that Ayton would easily have been the Open champion in 1885 but for his horrendous 11 that he took on the Road Hole. Contending that he remembered quite well what happened, Martin described every stroke. The only problem is that the actual records of the championships dredged up by historian Bobby Burnett and published in his 1990 history of the St. Andrews Open confirms that David Ayton returned a score of 89 in the first round and 84 in the final round for a total of 173. The winner, Bob Martin, returned a total score of 171. Thus, historian Burnett concludes that it would have required a miracle for Ayton to have suffered the indignity of an 11 at the Road Hole under these facts. Martin was simply mistaken.

No matter who is right on this historical point of interest, there is a lesson to be learned here. Whatever score Ayton made on the Road Hole that fateful day, surely David Ayton would agree that if it was not an 11, it sure felt like one!

22

THAT GREEDY LITTLE BUNKER

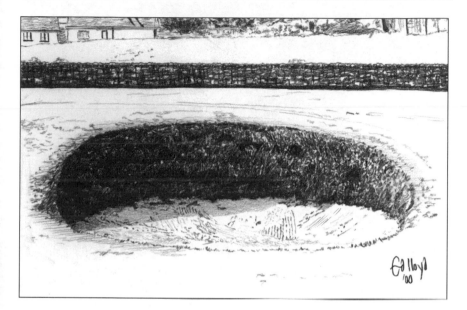

Bernard Darwin is celebrated as the dean of golf writers and historians. Darwin was an extravagant exponent of the well-crafted phrase. In 1908, Darwin left his post with the *Evening Standard* and became the longtime golf correspondent for *The Times*. He was also an accomplished golfer, becoming an original member of the Oxford and Cambridge Golfing Society and Captain of the Cambridge Golf Team. In 1909 and 1921, Darwin was a semifinalist in the British Amateur. In 1922, Darwin was sent by *The Times* to cover the 1922 Walker Cup Matches, played at the National Golf Links in New York. When Captain Robert Harris fell ill, Darwin was conscripted to replace him, and won his singles match. Darwin authored many books on golf, and among them he collaborated with painter Harry Rowntree to produce *The Golf Courses of the British Isles* in 1910. In the book, Darwin dubbed the Road Hole as the "Hole of Many Disastrous Memories." His description contained in *The Golf Courses of the British Isles* is well worth a second look:

The seventeenth hole has been more praised and more abused probably than any other hole in the world. It has been called unfair, and by many harder names as well; it has caused champions with a predilection for pitching rather than running to tear their hair; it has certainly ruined an infinite number of scores. Many

Bernard Darwin playing from The Road

like it, most respect it, and all fear it. First there is the tee-shot, with the possibility of slicing out-of-bounds into the stationmaster's garden or pulling into various bunkers on the left. Then comes the second, a shot which should not entail immediate disaster, but which is nevertheless of enormous importance as leading up to the third. Finally, there is the approach to that little plateau—in contrast to most of the St. Andrews greens, a horribly small and narrow one—that lies between a greedy little bunker on the one side and a brutally hard road on the other. It is so difficult as to make the boldest inclined to approach on the installment system, and yet no amount of caution can do away with the chance of disaster. There was a harrowing moment in the Championship of 1910 when Braid's ball lay in the little bunker under the green. Even if he got it safely out, it was practically certain he would be two strokes behind Duncan, with one round to go; if he did not get it out, or got it out too far and so on to the road, his chances would be terribly jeopardized. It was, as I say, an agonizing moment, but no one plays the heavy 'dunch' shot out of sand quite so surely as Braid. Down came the niblick, up spouted the sand, and out came the ball, to fall spent and lifeless close to the hole and out of reach of that cruel road.
It goes without saying that the Road Hole wouldn't be so fearsome if it were not for that greedy little bunker!

AH, WELL, THERE WE ARE

Henry Longhurst interviewing Bob Jones in 1958

Over the long history of golf broadcast journalism, one man cast the longest shadow. Henry Longhurst wrote for the *Sunday Times* and provided commentary for the BBC during the Open Championship and CBS during the Masters. Unlike some commentators who were hobbled by an unhealthy dose of acerbic sarcasm or overbearing omniscience, Longhurst (affectionately nicknamed "Longthirst" for obvious reasons) expressed his views with uncommon compassion, sensitivity, and insight. In the realm of golfing verbosity, Longhurst proposed that "less is more." A few words from Henry not only spoke volumes about the moment, but also precisely placed the event in the proper context of golf history. All in a single breath. It was a gift about which his admirers constantly marveled. Such as the defining

moment at the 16th hole of Oakland Hills in the 1972 PGA Championship in which Gary Player played a daring stroke to win his second title. Although he could have spoken for hours, Henry only said two words: "Staggering shot!" The pregnant silence which followed was deafening.

One of the most anguished moments in golf for players and spectators alike was covered by Henry during the 1970 Open Championship. The man from Cedartown, Georgia, Doug Sanders, was poised to collect the biggest title of his life when he bent over a putt which has variously been estimated at anywhere from three to five feet. Suddenly and uncharacteristically, Doug stopped, stooped over and brushed away a dark grass fragment, and then without regathering himself and reestablishing his stance, stabbed at the wee putt. He missed. Speaking eloquently for all of us who watched, Henry whispered under his breath, ".... but for the grace of God...."

Observers of the 1970 Open Championship were thankful that Longhurst was on hand at the Road Hole. When accomplished British golfer Brian Barnes placed his approach on the front left of the green, the task fell to Longhurst to explain the perils that the golfer faced. An accomplished player, Barnes figured prominently in the 1973 and 1979 Ryder Cup Matches, winning over 40% of his 26 individual matches. In 1981, he would set a record nine-hole score of 28 in the Haig Whiskey TPD Championship at Dalmahoy. Barnes well knew which was the business end of the golf club.

In a reverent tone, Henry began to explain the degree of difficulty in negotiating Barnes' putt to the top plateau where the hole was resident. The ball must be struck with sufficient but not excessive force to carry the concave depression where Barnes' ball lay. Too strong and the ball may carry over into the Road. It must be played to the right in order to ramp-up onto a narrow three-foot ledge. "If the ball should stray too far left of that intended line...." Then Henry's voice abruptly fell silent. He simply watched in unison with his viewers as the stroke unfolded. Barnes had sent his ball up the slope, and it was struggling mightily to climb onto the safety of the ledge. At first, it lost power. And then, it began to be consumed by the cavernous abyss. For several more seconds of silence befitting a funeral procession, the ball rolled around the bowl-shaped hollow which feeds into the carnivorous Road bunker. When the ball had at last been deposited with finality on the sandy bottom of the bunker, Henry delivered his eulogy: "Ah, well, there we are."

DON'T PLAY FOR THE HOLE

*From left to right: Cyril Tolley, Andrew Jamieson,
Watts Gunn, and Bobby Jones*

The second visit by Bobby Jones to Great Britain was in 1926 when the Walker Cup competition was scheduled at the Old Course. During the prior week, Jones was put out in the sixth round, four and three, by the exemplary play of Andrew Jamieson who was never over par and was one under on two occasions during the 15-hole match. Jones' opportunity to avenge his loss was presented in his Walker Cup foursomes competition with partner and fellow Atlantan, Watts Gunn, against Cyril Tolley and Jamieson. Jones was cautiously optimistic after returning a one-under-par performance in his lopsided victory over Tolley (12 and 11) in the singles matches.

Jones was understandably nervous about the fact that his partner, Watts, had never previously traveled outside the state of Georgia. But Jones persuaded Watts' father to allow sportswriter O.B. Keeler to chaperone Watts on the trip overseas with the Walker Cup Team. When first presented with the difficulty of the links courses of Great Britain, Watts was heard to remark, "You know this course wouldn't be so hard if it weren't for the wind." When Watts went to the Louvre Museum in

Watts Gunn—The "Southern Hurricane"

Paris and saw the Venus de Milo, he quipped, "I guess they didn't take enough exercise in those days. If those dames had played golf and tennis and done some swimming and learned the Charleston, they would have been a lot easier to look at." Upon seeing the Eiffel Tower, Watts added, "Of course it has never tipped over, but this would be the time that it would tip over. Why, listen—I bet I'm the only person in Paris that stepped on a piece of chewing gum today. They don't chew more than two pieces a week in Paris."

Watts played well enough in his singles match against Lord Lurgan (W.G. Brownlow). At a critical juncture in the match, Watts successfully negotiated a stymie to win the hole. Lord Lurgan was so staggered that Watts won the next five holes in the match. When told that Lord Lurgan was a musician, Watts replied, "I don't know if he can play a violin, but he made some music with a brassie at the 8th hole, and the way he rings the bell with a putter, he must be a Swiss!" Jones' concern about Watts' capacity to withstand the pressure was exacerbated when Watts discovered that his

St. Andrews caddie had left five of his favorite clubs behind when he had started out the match. All Watts could get out of the caddie was, "Ye have no need for so many!" His caddie was right. On the 13th green, Watts holed a 120-foot putt (the next year Jones sank a putt of equal length on the fifth green which is shared with the 13th). The spirited match then produced one of the most "terrifying bits of golf [Jones] ever saw." In an article penned by Jones and published the next day he recounted the experience:

Watts Gunn and I collaborated at this same hole in one of the most terrifying bits of golf I have ever seen. It was in the Walker Cup matches last year and we were playing Tolley and Jamieson in the Scotch foursomes, which means each partner plays alternate strokes on the same ball. Watts and Jamieson were driving at the seventeenth. The drive here is supposed to go straight over the middle of a barn which is out-of-bounds. Watts just got over, while Jamieson hit the building plump in the middle and Tolley had to play three off the tee. Cyril, made cautious by his partner's mistake, pulled his drive over into the second fairway. It was now my turn and I played a conservative spoon shot short of and in front of the green. Jamieson topped the fourth for his team and Tolley, in a heroic effort to reach the green, went over into the road. That was five for our opponents and being in the road they would do well to go down in eight.

Watts and I looked certain to win the hole. But nothing is ever certain on the seventeenth at St. Andrews. Watts had to play a run-up to the very narrow green between the bunker on one side and the road on the other, and he shanked it into the road. Now we were in the road in three, they in five.

Jamieson played a beautiful shot up twelve feet from the hole. That looked bad for us, for our ball was lying in the hard road, the hole was only fifteen or twenty feet away, the green was dry, and the terrible bunker was just beyond the flag. Watts and I put our heads togther and indulged in a little mental arithmetic. We finally decided that if I should play down toward the brook behind the green, Watts could pitch back on so that two putts would give us a seven and a halve if Tolley holed his putt. We felt we would be thankful for anything now. We did get our seven. Tolley rimmed the long one, and we won the hole, but not until we had used up all our shots and most of the little brains we had.

The match ended in favor of the Atlantans, four and three.

Bob Jones and Roger Wethered

JOHN HENRY'S ENEMY

A prominent member of "The Great Triumvirate" was John Henry Taylor. Taylor won the first of his five Open Championships at the age of 23 in 1894 playing a gutta-percha ball on the links at Sandwich. He used a rubber ball to win his fifth Open Championship in 1913, which was 19 years later. Not only did Taylor win five Open Championships over a 19-year span, but he was also runner-up five times. Taylor was successful at home and abroad as well. He won two French Open Championships and one German Open. He also won two News of the World Championships, now called the British PGA. Taylor also traveled to the United States, where he was runner-up in the U.S. Open in 1900, losing by two strokes to Harry Vardon.

John Henry had one great enemy in his golfing career. It was the Road Hole at St. Andrews. Taylor was an extravagant admirer of pitching his ball with the mashie iron, arguing that golf was a game that was played in the air, not on the ground. In articles authored for the *Golfing Press*, Taylor did not mean that golfers should not play pitch shots when the circumstances called for it. He conceded that certain shots could be "Too Muckle up in the air" and they could be "Too Muckle along the gr'und." John Henry was very skilled at the run-up shot which required the player to carefully survey the topography of the ground over which the ball must run. But given a choice, Taylor argued that the pitch shot was perhaps easier, although his view was tainted by the fact that he was a master of that stroke.

One of Taylor's close friends and rivals was Andra Kirkaldy of St. Andrews. Unlike Taylor, Kirkaldy was a fervent proponent of the run-up shot over the pitch. The argument between the two players ultimately became public knowledge. One newspaper cartoonist drew a caricature of Kirkaldy "pitching" John Henry into the air from the toe of his boot. It was supposed to satirize a perfect mashie shot, portraying Taylor to have been the ball and Kirkaldy's boot to be the clubhead. John Henry was not particularly amused.

When John Henry came to the Road Hole in the 1905 Open at St. Andrews, his second stroke was in the middle of the fairway. He was once again faced with the difficult choice of whether to pitch the ball or run it up to the green. The last time he had seen a shot played from that exact position was his friend, Kirkaldy, in a 50-pound challenge match played between the two. Kirkaldy played a deft run up

John Henry Taylor and Bob Jones

along the hollow just to the right of the Road Bunker. The stroke was played per-fectly, curling along the edge of the hollow onto the top plateau where the flagstick was located. But John Henry did not profit by the example set for him by Kirkaldy.

Instead, Taylor attempted his favorite pitching shot. Disaster struck. The ball bit into the bank of the hollow, and was gathered into the Road Bunker. He took nine strokes to hole out, and lost by five strokes to James Braid.

After the championship, John Henry was still rankled by his collapse at the Road Hole. In discussing the matter with Kirkaldy, they decided to walk over to the 17th and reconstruct in their minds how such a cruel fate could be visited upon such a skilled player. Kirkaldy went to the exact scene of the crime, and dropped several practice balls. He was able to play several run-up strokes through the hollow, and finish very near to the flagstick. Kirkaldy then handed the club to Taylor for a try. On each of a half-dozen strokes, Taylor ran one ball after the other close to the hole where they nestled together. With an air of resignation, Taylor turned to Kirkaldy and confessed: "There are some times to pitch and times not to pitch. I 'pitched' that championship away."

NEVER SAY NEVER

An accomplished American Walker Cup player who played in the 1930 and 1936 Walker Cup matches was George Voigt. In 1930, Voigt reached the semifinals against Bob Jones in the British Amateur. The two waged an epic battle over the first nine holes. By the 13th hole, however, Voigt's mastery with iron clubs gave him an unexpected two-hole advantage over Jones. And therein lies a story. A fable well known to natives of St. Andrews said that a golfer who is "two up and five to play never wins his match." This maxim was whispered among at least a dozen spectators on the 14th tee as Voigt prepared to drive his ball.

The conditions up to that point had been unusually benign, but at that moment a fresh breeze suddenly blew from left to right. The only problem was that Voigt could not feel the breeze because the spectators had crowded around the tee insulating him from gauging the force of the wind. Sadly for George, the line he had selected down the right side, along the out-of-bounds wall, was the wrong one under the circumstances. Voigt's ball drifted out-of-bounds and he was forced to play another ball from the tee, thereby losing the hole. After halving the 15th, Voigt again chose the wrong line on his drive, when his ball bounded into the "Principal's Nose" bunker. That squared the match coming to the treacherous Road Hole.

Both players eschewed the risk of driving over the corner of the Stationmaster's garden, and instead both played to the left of the fairway. Voigt then chose to gamble. He played a risky stroke to the front edge of the green, precariously flirting with the road bunker. Jones played a more conservative iron shot, fully 20 yards in front of the green, thus placing a premium on his approach. Using his putter, Voigt deftly hit the bank, passed the cavernous slope which acts like a magnet in drawing balls into the bunker. He nearly holed out for a three and finished inches from the cup for a sure four. Jones' run-up shot was indifferently played, leaving him with a desperate 18-foot putt for a halve. Jones stalked the "do or die putt" from every angle. And then he did what few thought possible. He rendered a fatal psychological blow to Voigt by sinking the putt. On the 18th, Voigt was again victimized. This time by the Valley of Sin. And Jones was able to fulfill his destiny of the Grand Slam. Some commentators have written that Jones never would have achieved his ambition but for that 18-foot putt on the Road Hole against George Voigt.

Bob Jones vs. Cyril Tolley (1930)

Bob Jones vs. Roger Wethered (1930)

BILLIARD GOLF

On his way to the Grand Slam, Bob Jones invented a new way to play the Road Hole during his controversial match with Cyril Tolley in the Amateur Championship. None of Bob's matches at St. Andrews in 1930 would be separated by more than a couple of strokes, and the match with Cyril Tolley was no exception. Bernard Darwin observed that *"every man, woman, and child in St. Andrews"* was on hand to see which titan of golf could master the gale that masqueraded as "fresh breeze." It blew the sand out of the bunkers while spectators took refuge in the sand hills between shots. With the wind at their backs the two players could drive the green at the ninth and were able to drive over the green at the 314-yard 12th. Going against the wind at the short 11th, however, neither player could gauge the shot— Tolley falling short of the green and Jones long. Every putt was tainted with treachery and emphasized the need to measure not only the quickness of the surface but also the effect of the wind itself. The seesaw battle produced six occasions upon which Bob took the lead, accompanied by six efforts by Tolley to square the match. Then the contestants reached the Road Hole all level and set the stage for a controversy that is today still fodder for lively debate.

Cyril slightly outdrove Bob and had a second to the green less obstructed by the deadly bunker guarding the left of the steeply sloping green. Bob was positioned on the left of the fairway and was only briefly tempted with a direct shot to the flag over that same bunker. Bob had seldom before tempted himself with the daring second over the Road Bunker and in 1927 had four times played short of the green and relied on a wee pitch to collect his 4. The big difference in 1930 was the gale-force wind and marbletop-fast greens which dictated a change in strategy.

Bob decided that a direct shot to the green put the road into play, should the shot be exaggerated with adrenaline. His best recourse would be to play up the left side of the green adjacent to the 18th tee while mindful of the need to be past the Road Bunker. Bob could then play his approach without hindrance of the Road Bunker. Bob climbed a hillock and waved the marshals to move the crowd back away from the intended flight line. After he was satisfied that the crowd could move back no further, Bob struck a mashie 4-iron a bit stronger than needed and the ball landed into the crowd, struck a spectator, and was deflected back to the top edge of the green. Some observers asserted that the shot was intentionally played into the crowd.

Chick Evans playing from The Road

One eyewitness to the match, Harry Andrew, wrote a 1957 article in the *Glasgow Sunday Express* entitled "Why Bobby Jones Aimed to Hit the Crowd." Mr. Andrew remembered the incident as follows:

And so to the dreaded Road Hole with two to play and the issue as wide open as ever. Tolley's second finished behind the bunker guarding the green. Jones saw this before he, too, had to play. He went into a huddle with his famous old caddie, Jock MacIntyre. In the distance was lined 10 deep right around the green.

Said Jones: 'Can I trust the crowd?'

Replied MacIntyre: 'Man, they canna move.'

So the American hit a low flying iron shot straight at the crowd at the back of the green. The ball landed on the green, bounced once, hit a spectator on the chest—and rebounded to land 12 feet from the flag!

Incidentally, officials took prompt note of Jones' perfectly legal tactics—and since that championship, crowds have been made to stay behind the wall.

However, later in his same article, Mr. Andrew provides a refutation of his own thesis that Jones intentionally aimed to hit the crowd for strategic reasons. Mr. Andrew reports his then-recent interview with Tolley on the match:

I had only myself to blame against Jones—and it was a bad second shot that beat me, much more than the stymie.

Tolley, of course, is still full of memories of the wonderful match. He recalled to me that they had taken 4 hours 35 minutes to play the 19 holes—thanks to the crowd antics.

'I hit the crowd five times,' he said. 'Bob did it eight times. And we actually went through another match at the 16th without knowing that they were playing the hole! Have any regrets? Not a one. I'm glad Bob won his four titles that year. But at St. Andrews my job was to beat him. I didn't and that's all there is to it. He's a grand chap and I'll always remember that scrap.'

Mr. Andrew surely "mythed" the point. If both players hit the crowd with 134 separately played strokes, it should not be reasonably concluded that only one of these was intentional and the remainder were simply inadvertent.

Bob insisted that his efforts to move the spectators back was proof enough that he never planned a ricochet against the crowd. Everyone agrees that there was genius in that approach. Tolley's second shot was pulled slightly and came to rest to the left of the green with the devilish Road Bunker intervening. Cyril next played a deft pitch over the Road Bunker to the hole. The pitch was *"bravely judged so that it trembled momentarily on the edge of the bunker before trickling down a foot from the hole."*

Bob later acknowledged that Tolley's third shot *"has never been surpassed for exquisitely beautiful execution."* Tolley himself agreed it was the finest shot of his life. Both 17 and 18 were halved, taking the match to the 19th hole. Each player was understandably exhausted. Nevertheless, the match did end in Bob's favor with the assistance of a stymie. Tolley's second shot had ended left of the green, and his chip was just inside Bob's 10-foot birdie putt. The birdie failed in its effort, but its position blocking the hole frustrated Tolley from putting directly toward it.

Following the Jones' incident, the crowd control policies were changed and spectators were sequestered away from the 18th tee where Jones' ball had landed. After all, the game is golf, not billiards.

Henry Cotton and Walter Hagen

OH DEAR!

Henry Cotton became a professional golfer at the tender age of 17. Some say that he was the greatest British professional since Harry Vardon. Cotton was certainly as well-loved. After 10 years of American domination of the British Open Championship, Cotton rescued the trophy at Sandwich in 1934 and became an instant celebrity on the international golfing stage. Henry proved that it was not a fluke by winning twice again in 1937 (Carnoustie) and 1948 (Muirfield). Cotton's second round 65 in the 1934 Open Championship remained the lowest round until 1977. To commemorate the record round, Dunlop invented a special ball in Henry's honor dubbed the "Dunlop 65." Not only did Cotton win 35 titles, but he also served as Captain of the 1947 and 1953 British Ryder Cup teams. Cotton was knighted in 1987 for his contributions to golf.

The abiding lesson that Cotton learned from playing St. Andrews was "humility." He explained what he meant:

I've done everything at St. Andrews in major events—popped one into the Swilcan Burn before the first green; been in the deep bunker at the 11th, and had an impossible lie... I've been out-of-bounds at the 14th, over the wall when seven under fours, and going like a dream to crush with a seven for the hole. I've been, of course, in Hell Bunker with a second shot which just failed to make it. At the 16th, I've been in the "Principal's Nose" and dropped another shot... I've been - oh dear!—three under on the 17th tee several times and then hit one onto the Road.

    *   *   *

I do not get cross anymore when young golfers claim they detest the place. I just feel sorry that they are so ignorant and unappreciative of what they have inherited—but I'm sure most of these, as they grow older, learn to understand that golf is a dull game when every hole plays the same way every day. At St. Andrews you never know what to expect. I can't say more than I just love the place.

Tom Watson playing from near the wall of the Road in 1984.

WRONG-WRONG-WRONG

If ever a player mastered the subtleties of links style golf in Great Britain, he is Tom Watson. On five occasions Watson earned the title of "Champion Golfer of the Year" in Great Britain by winning the Open Championship (1975, 1977, 1980, 1982, 1983). He has also won two Masters championships (1977, 1981) and the 1982 U.S. Open Championship. Watson has not prevented his innermost desire from being made public. That fictional title is to win a Scottish Slam. That is, to win the Open Championship at each and every venue in Scotland. The only missing piece of the puzzle for Watson is a victory at St. Andrews. Perhaps his best opportunity to achieve that dream was presented in the 1984 Open Championship. Coming to the final round, Watson and Australian Ian Baker-Finch led the field by two over the sanguine Spaniard, Seve Ballesteros, and the German, Bernhard Langer. Except for his play on the Road Hole, Seve seemed poised to win. But in the first three rounds he bogeyed the Road Hole by driving his tee shot too far to the left. Apparently he had not healed the emotional wound inflicted by slicing his tee shot out-of-bounds to lose the 1978 Open. Once he had touched the hot coals of the boundary on the right of the Road Hole, he resolved never to repeat the blunder. Seve was happy with his scores, saying, "I make three 5s now—it's par!" Then he promised in his press interview, "I make four tomorro—if not, I play Monday." True to his word, playing in front of Watson, Ballesteros again drove to the left rough, leaving a 200-yard shot to the flagstick. He told his caddic, "I am not worried about the drive, it is the second shot that is most important." Seve then hit a number six-iron, which landed short of the green and bounced safely onto the front edge, 35-feet from the hole. His birdie putt narrowly missed by two inches and he left the green tied with Watson at 11 under par.

Whereas Seve hit his drive on the wrong side of the fairway for the best approach, Watson smote his ball on the far right side for the easiest approach. At least that was Watson's intent. When he struck the tee shot, however, it appeared at first glance that he had bitten off more than he could chew. Ordinarily, Watson has a favorite target, being the sign on the faux black sheds which reads "Old Course Golf & Country Club." Watson's ideal line is to aim for the "C" in "Club." (Today the sign reads "St. Andrews Old Course Hotel.") At first he thought he missed his mark. Standing momentarily like a soldier at attention, he slowly raised his arms and

hunched his shoulders as if to signal that he could not vouch that his ball was in play. By this gesture, he was asking the forecaddies if they could confirm whether or not his ball was indeed out-of-bounds. His furled forehead was soon relieved when he saw the signal that his ball was in play. In fact, it was almost in perfect position 190 yards away from the hole and with a pristine view of the green. That's when he hit the wrong club, at the wrong time and on the wrong hole. Incredibly, it was three wrongs in a row.

Whereas Seve hit a six-iron, Watson chose a number two-iron. Against a slight breeze he settled in his stance over the ball. About that same time an ominous roar from the crowd on No. 18 cascaded down the vista that reached to where Watson was standing. The message was clear—Seve had stuck his approach within birdie range on the home hole. And a greater sense of urgency surrounded Watson at that moment. For whatever reason, he pushed the shot badly. Hitting the back edge of the green, his ball bounced into the wall adjoining the Road but it did not hit one of the stones comprising the wall. Slow-motion films of the shot show that it hit the soft mortar holding the stones together. Thus, the ball did not violently rebound off the stone wall. It merely dropped lifelessly at a distance that was sure to abbreviate and annoy Watson's next stroke. After surveying his plight, Watson fidgeted nervously over his ball, with the added indignity of not being permitted to sole his club in the hazard. Although the word should not be used in polite company, it must be said that Watson "hacked" his third stroke onto the green. As he contemplated salvaging his putt for a four, another roar rolled down the 18th fairway. The Spaniard had thrust his sword into the neck of the bull with a three at the home hole. With his face a study in resignation, Watson's 30-foot putt eased past the hole, taking with it any reasonable hope to catch Seve. He would have to hole in two on the 18th. It had been done before. Just once, by Tom Duncan, professional at Falkirk Tryst Club. And it has been done since by Nick Faldo in the 1990 Open. But it would require exactly the right shot with the right club at the right time. Sadly, for Watson at this moment in history, three wrongs could not make a right.

In December 1989, *Golf World* conducted a poll of the professional players to determine the single stroke they would most like to replay in their careers. As one might suspect, Watson nominated his 2-iron at the Road Hole in 1984.

DAVID MARSH'S DAGGER

The seventh occasion upon which St. Andrews hosted the Walker Cup Matches was in 1971. Prior matches were held in 1923, 1926, 1934, 1938, 1947, and 1955. The British Isles first won the competition in 1938 against a talented American invasion led by that year's British Amateur Champion Charlie Yates. The next occasion was in 1971 when St. Andrews hosted the 50th Anniversary of the inaugural 1921 Informal Matches contested at Hoylake.

In the singles matches on the final afternoon, Great Britain made a commanding statement in winning six singles. Two were won on the 17th green, and four were won on the last green. The outcome hung in the balance of one match. That veritable sword of Damocles was poised directly over the singles match convened at the Road Hole between David Marsh and American, Bill Hyndman. He was the same Bill Hyndman who made the magical stroke described by Bobby Jones as perhaps the greatest he ever saw during the 1958 World Amateur Team Championship. But that was another day.

Marsh had several factors that militated against his chances for success. First, he had driven his ball to the left of the fairway, leaving him 220 yards with a fresh breeze blowing from the Road on the right toward the Road Bunker on the left. The margin for error was so slender a slight pull or push would have visited dire consequences on Marsh's chances. At that moment, he stood one-up on Hyndman and desperately needed to halve the hole and become dormie to win the cup. Marsh's anxiety was prolonged by the agony of having to wait until the match ahead had cleared the green.

Hyndman struck his approach which just failed to mount the bank of the hillock, and consequently finished its journey at the front. Marsh selected a number three-iron and intended to land his ball on the front right of the green, hoping it would take the slope and run onto the top plateau. The ominous murmur of those excited spectators who surrounded the green, lined the fairway, and even populated the balcony of the Old Course Hotel, fell eerily silent. Marsh struck his ball with vigor, and it traveled the exact path he had designed. The stroke stuck a dagger into the heart of America's hopes, and procured yet a second victory for Great Britain and Ireland at St. Andrews.

43

*"No hole in existence has been the innocent cause of
so many opprobrious epithets and language of so
lurid hue as the Road Hole," wrote Harold Hilton.*

GOOD GOD!

One player who was almost fatally victimized by the Road Hole but lived to tell the tale was Harold Hilton. With his contemporary, John Ball, Jr., Hilton learned his golf over the venerable Hoylake Links of the Royal Liverpool Golf Club. Hilton assembled a spectacular golfing record playing as an Amateur. He won two Open Championships, four British Amateur Championships, and one U.S. Amateur Championship from 1892 to 1913. In 1911, he became the first player ever to win both the British Amateur and the U.S. Amateur Championships in the same year. Hilton was also an accomplished golf writer, serving as golf editor of *Golf Monthly* for many years.

Hilton made no bones about his dislike for the Road Hole when he wrote: "No hole in existence has been the innocent cause of so many opprobrious epithets and language of so lurid hue as the Road Hole."

In his 33 appearances in the British Amateur Championship, Hilton twice won the title at St. Andrews (1901, 1913) and was runner-up in 1891. His victory in 1901 was the first successful defense of that title since 1887, and the last until Lawson Little repeated the feat in 1935. The fact that Hilton has harbored such ill will toward the Road Hole is some indication of just how badly the wits were scared out of him on those few occasions he played it.

In the 1901 Championship, Hilton played Horace G. Hutchinson in the semifinal match. After Hutchinson presented Hilton with the first three holes, he found his form and crawled back to one-up with five holes to play. Hilton then capitalized on Hutchinson's errors and reached the Road Hole two holes up in the match. Hilton decided to play to the extreme left from the tee, while avoiding going over the black sheds at all costs. He had been persuaded by Andrew Kirkaldy that the ideal strategy, especially with a strong prevailing wind, was to play left of the Road Bunker. The hole played significantly longer in those days of the hickory shaft. Hilton's drive and second shot were played down the left side. Then he employed his newly acquired aluminum spoon (today's metal woods are simply a revival of old technology) and landed his ball faithfully on the green. The match with Hutchinson was over.

Hilton then set out to dispatch grizzled veteran, John Low, who knew the Old Course like the back of his hand. Hilton played well in the early going, earning a five-hole advantage in the afternoon of the second round. But it evaporated as quickly as one could say "Road Hole."

The match was level when Hilton and Low stood on the 17th tee. The exuberant hometown crowd of Low supporters added salt to Hilton's wound when they nearly knocked Hilton on his butt, shouting, "We'll teach these bloody Englishmen!" Steeling his resolve with determination rather than anger, Hilton replied under his breath, "Will you now?" He played one cracking shot down the left side off the tee, and another down the left from the fairway. The only problem was that he had hooked his second shot more toward the home hole. Low had placed his third stroke on the left edge of the Road Bunker, and would be forced to negotiate the bunker on his next shot. There was a stiff breeze directly in Hilton's face, so he asked his caddie if he could reach the Road with his third shot. "Doubtful," said the caddie. So Hilton took his driver and let out the shaft. It was a splendid shot indeed. The ball held up in the air momentarily and then softly landed on the green and stayed. In a desperate "do or die" pitch, Low's next stroke over the bunker finished in the Road. It proved to be Hilton's margin of victory.

The Road Hole also proved to be pivotal in Hilton's 1913 Amateur Championship victory. His final match against Robert Harris was won in a "cakewalk" by a lopsided margin of six and five. The important spadework was done in the early match with the American champion of Massachusetts, Heinrich Schmidt. Schmidt's reputation had preceded his arrival to St. Andrews. Darwin's column in *The Times* sounded the warning alarm for his British brethren: "The tragedy of Mr. Travis is likely to be re-enacted sooner than we either like or expect." In his inimitable style, Darwin was forecasting that an American victory such as the first one inflicted by Walter Travis in 1904 could easily be repeated if the British players were not "en garde." Darwin was right.

The first hole set the tone for the entire match. Hilton routinely put his approach shot on the green and putted stone dead for a par. It's a good thing Hilton is patient. Because Schmidt acted as though he was making a deadman's walk to the gallows. With excruciating deliberation that rendered the rule on playing with "undue delay" an anachronism, Schmidt looked at his lengthy putt from every direction on the compass. Then he appeared to wear himself out with a frenetic number of practice strokes. He followed that with another professorial examination of the line. Then, before any of the spectators were compelled to burst forth with the encouragement, "Would you please play the stroke!" Schmidt banged his ball

into the middle of the hole for a birdie. Suffice it to say for poor Hilton that the match did not proceed with any greater dispatch. As Darwin once sagely wrote, "Golf is not a funeral, though both can be sad things."

By the time they reached the Road Hole, the match was all square. Schmidt took four strokes to get on the green. Advantage Hilton. Instead of playing to the left this time, Hilton was just short and to the right on his second stroke. He took his putter and rapped his ball in the equator. The ball jumped and gyrated over the remaining fairway, which took much of the speed off its journey. Then the ball attempted to climb a steep slope but it soon became obvious that it was not going to make it. Hilton's ball soon curled to the left and was gathered into the bosom of the Road Bunker. As the ball made its inglorious exit from the rabbitey turf, one Scottish spectator cried in anguish, "Good God!" The genuine tone of the lament and its finality was such that it caused most of the gallery, including Hilton, to dissolve in laughter. Whereas the tension of the match had made Hilton taut as a banjo string, the laughter permitted him to relax just for a moment. After composing himself, Hilton marched into the beastly bunker as resolutely as did the 600 into the Valley of Death. He then played a brave stroke, depositing his ball back onto the putting surface. Though the hole was halved, the psychological momentum seemed from that point onward to favor Hilton. The match was won on the first extra hole, where Hilton turned the tables on his opponent and this time made his winning birdie putt.

Bob Jones and Robert Harris

MARK OF THE FOOL

The 1925 British Amateur Champion was Robert Harris. Harris was also runner-up in the 1913 Amateur at St. Andrews and the 1923 Amateur at Deal. In 1926, he was put out of the fifth round of the Championship at Muirfield by Bobby Jones. In his book *Sixty Years of Golf* published in 1953, Harris reviewed the virtues of the Road Hole:

> *The seventeenth hole, or "Stationmaster's Garden," comes at the right place in a needle match. This is a nerve tester in its play from start to finish. No player ever stands on the tee here facing the black sheds without having to suppress a small tremor. It takes years of tolerance and failure to make modern golfers understand this is a golf hole. It is reviled, scoffed at once in a way, then it comes to be feared, cursed with vehemence as being stupid and unfair, but golfers who have played it, in course of time learn all about it. Those who haven't must see it to believe it.*
>
> *All its lurking dangers loom up after a misplaced shot: the player must play for position, a yard or two away from the required spot causes a scratching of the head, in consultation with the caddie. The insouciance or bravado of the player who looks at the chart for distance in yards and then goes for the green in two, shows the mark of the fool. Fives, sixes, sevens, and eights are much more frequent scores at this hole than threes. Overambitious players in medal play with a five and a four to win have sliced twice out-of-bounds and retired from the contest. My opponent in a Walker Cup match obliged once in a similar unguarded moment. Many a match has been finished by the player one down here slicing to glory over the sheds, or the leader by trying to bite off too much loses his winning advantage.*

If there was one match that stuck in Harris' craw, it was his ouster at the Road Hole by Ernest Holderness in the 1924 Amateur Championship. Before the match, Harris' confidence was buoyed by the fact that he had beaten Holderness in the International Matches at Deal the year before. Moreover, Harris thought he had more experience at St. Andrews than his opponent. He had been in the semifinal match in 1907 and reached the final in 1913, when he was vanquished by Hilton.

Besides, St. Andrews was his favorite course. But Harris suffered a crack in the armor when he three-putted the 15th green. The coup de grâce was administered on the Road Hole when Holderness exhibited the "impertinence" to pitch his third stroke onto the Road Hole green, get a four, and beat Harris by a margin of two to one. Impertinence, indeed!

CARD WRECKER

By 1930, the championship that Bob Jones most wanted to win was the British Amateur. After battling his way through the preliminary rounds, Jones faced a 36-hole final match against 1923 Amateur Champion Roger Wethered. The Saturday contest was also a holiday, and consequently, enormous crowds gathered for the closing contest — about 6,000 persons in the morning and almost 15,000 in the afternoon. "Motorcars streamed into the city from all quarters," the *St. Andrews Citizen* reported. "Thousands arrived by rail, and the various buses were packed."

A most peculiar thing happened on the first tee before the match started. Francis Ouimet was standing very close to Bobby, and as the gallery settled in, an official of the R&A made a very curious observation: "Golf has been played at St. Andrews for over 100 years. During that time, every one of the greatest golfers in the world has at some time or other played The Old Course. Wonderful scores have been made, but no one has ever been able to play a round without having at least one five on his card." Jones pursed his lips tightly, but did not say a word. After a spirited opening nine holes of the match, the players found themselves level after each going out in 35 strokes. Then Jones shifted into a higher gear. Standing on the 17th tee, Jones was five up in the morning round with only two remaining holes.

Both players drove in perfect position in the fairway. Then Wethered gambled with a grand spoon shot that found its way onto the putting surface. Jones responded with a spoon shot that drew a shade too much and landed in the Road Bunker. Much of the sand had been blown out of the bunker, which made an explosion shot extremely risky. The marbletop-fast green sloped precipitously away toward the road. Although he was not more than 15 or 20 feet from the hole, Jones was hobbled by his choices. Francis Ouimet carefully watched as Jones swung his punch-faced Hendry & Bishop miter brand niblick slowly back and then cut the legs out from underneath the ball, which just barely cleared the top of the bunker wall. The ball hit on the downslope and then began to tremble, twist, and squirm from the extreme backspin Jones had imparted with that deft stroke. As the ball hit the downslope, it abruptly abbreviated its speed and then leaked slowly past the hole while ending its journey only two feet away. A grizzled St. Andrews professional told Ouimet it was the finest shot he had ever seen. Francis concurred, "What a shot!"

After Wethered two-putted from 18 feet, it was Jones' turn to finish the task. In

51

an uncharacteristic fashion, however, Jones quickly swung his feet around, took his stance and rushed to tap the ball into the hole. You wouldn't believe it. He missed. The great Jones. From two feet. The spectators, including Ouimet, were horrified.

Slowly, but surely, Jones' temperature began to rise from his neck to his cap. He furiously smashed his drive a prodigious distance up the 18th fairway. He won that hole with a four and finished with a medal score of 71 that gave him a four-up advantage

After finishing the round, Jones crossed the street and went into his room at the Grand Hotel with Ouimet trailing behind. Jones looked at his friend Francis with wild-eyed disgust. Ouimet could not understand why Jones was so upset, "What in the world has got into you, Bobby? You were four up." Jones bitterly replied, "Did you hear what that official said on the first tee? And I had to miss a two-foot putt to be the first man to play St. Andrews without taking a five." The Road Hole had again proved to be a card wrecker.

Don't feel too sorry for Jones, though. He dispatched Wethered on the 12th hole in the afternoon with the margin at seven and six. His medal score was two-under fours. And he finally captured the one championship he wanted to win more than any other. Road Hole be damned.

Furthermore, Jones would possibly be relieved today with the knowledge that the curse of the "fiveless card" was mercifully broken in the Centenary Open. Peter Alliss scored a marvelous 66 in 1960, and he didn't have a single five on his card.

A LITTLE LOCAL KNOWLEDGE

Francis Ouimet was one of the first Americans to discover the charm and genius of the Old Course at St. Andrews. As a 19-year-old boy, Ouimet was the first American amateur to capture the U.S. Open in a 1913 playoff against the legendary Ted Ray and Harry Vardon. In 1914, he won the U.S. Amateur at East Kwanok Country Club in Vermont, and in 1931, he added the U.S. Amateur Championship contested at Beverly C.C. in Chicago. He was the first American to be elected captain of the Royal & Ancient Golf Club in 1951.

In the 1923 Walker Cup Matches, Ouimet learned that a little local knowledge could go a long way at the Road Hole. He was paired against reigning British Amateur Champion Roger Wethered in his singles match. Ouimet came to the Road Hole one down in the match. In his biography, *A Game of Golf*, Francis described Wethered's successful strategy:

Then we came to the terrible seventeenth. This is par five, but, like the fourteenth, reachable in two. The fact that you can get home in two does not mean a thing, because there are so many dangers trying for the green that it is hardly worth the effort. We had two good tee shots. I played an iron, a safety-first sort of stroke, that could get me to the front edge and no farther. That is where my ball ended. Wethered, who knew the St. Andrews course like a book, deliberately played to the left beyond the little trap guarding the green and onto the eighteenth tee. I did not understand why he should do such a thing, but it did not take me long to find out his reason. When we arrived at our balls, I was left with a nasty approach putt up over a steep incline, a shot I abhor, whereas Roger had a nice place from which to roll his ball to the hole with nothing dangerous in the way. I putted and put my ball eight or ten inches from the cup. Wethered putted again from off the green, got inside, and that hole was halved.

On the End hole, Wethered's putt finished by blocking the hole by half the diameter of the ball. Ouimet's ball skimmed barely into the hole for a three, which to his relief and astonishment halved the match. Ouimet had played the last three holes three under par, had won two of them, had tied the course record with a 70, and used up all his resources in the process. On the other hand, Wethered only needed a little local knowledge.

53

***What I like about the Old Course is that you play a very good shot
and find yourself in a very bad place.*** George Duncan made three
at 17 in the 1922 Daily Mail Tournament placing his spoon second
shot only a foot from the flagstick.

AND THEY SAY THIS IS A TOUGH HOLE!

In the summer of 1990, Dr. Benjamin Dowdey sojourned to Scotland to play in the British Amateur at Muirfield. After concentrating on his practice in emergency medicine, Dr. Dowdey first picked up a golf club in his late 20s and made himself into a scratch player. But in this Amateur, he could not quite cajole his putter into behaving properly, taking many more putts than were allowed for a player to make the cut that year. With a little time on his hands, Dr. Dowdey traveled north to visit the Royal & Ancient Golf Club of St. Andrews, of which he is a member. Dr. Dowdey explained to hall porter, Tom Wallace, his travails at Muirfield and inquired whether there might be a game for him on the Old Course. Soon thereafter, on June 7, 1990, Dr. Dowdey joined Tim and Carl Fitzgerald from New York City first off the tee in the morning. The Fitzgeralds were a father and son team who had never before experienced the majesty of the Old Course. So Dr. Dowdey was a valuable historian to them in explaining the features seen at the home of golf. The history lesson did not necessarily interfere with Dr. Dowdey's fine golf either. He was one over par through the 16th hole. By way of further introduction to Dr. Dowdey's golfing skills, it might be mentioned that he is the only American ever to reach the finals of the Carnegie Shield Competition at the Royal Dornoch Golf Club. But that is another story.

There is one aspect of the Old Course that was well known to the Fitzgeralds. They knew that the Road Hole was the most formidable challenge in the world of golf. And they were eagerly anticipating that august moment when they stepped onto the 17th tee. But never could they have guessed that they would eyewitness a singular episode of golfing lore.

As a veteran player on the Old Course, Dr. Dowdey made his share of par 4s by playing safely to the front right of the green and taking his chances from there. Occasionally, he had been blessed with a birdie and, of course, was cursed with other scores as well.

Dr. Dowdey struck his drive well, but to the right of the "safe" line over the black sheds. "I think it may be in the breakfast nook of the hotel," he told his playing companions. But rounding the corner his ball was in good position on the right edge of the fairway. He then struck a four-iron flush toward the flagstick, which was posi-

tioned in the middle of the top tier of the green. His ball hit on the front and rolled up the steep bank, disappearing from sight. He thought to himself that it might even be a good shot. Fitzgerald, the younger, was positioned 100 yards ahead and to the left of the good doctor, which provided him a better visual vantage point. He began to wave his arms and shout, "The ball went in the hole." Dr. Dowdey simply smiled. *That kind of thing doesn't happen here. What the boy really means is just that the ball has rolled over the slope and out of sight. He's simply mistaken.*

But as the group approached the green, it was obvious that the ball was wedged between the flagstick and the hole. And then spontaneously it disappeared completely from sight. The Fitzgeralds and the caddies began shouts of jubilation. Dr. Dowdey was quietly stunned. Immediately behind the green, several spectators were standing on the Road and stoically watched the scene unfold. After the ball was retrieved from the hole, one spectator muttered aloud, "And they say this is a tough hole."

After finishing in a fine 71, Dr. Dowdey and his companions repaired to the R&A clubhouse, where the Fitzgeralds excitedly shared the news with hall porter, Tom Wallace. Wallace simply turned to Dr. Dowdey and observed, "If you had just done that at Muirfield, Doctor, you wouldn't have missed the cut."

THE BRASH AMERICAN

Walter Hagen

One brash caddie who supported his brazen and dashing style with a singular golfing record was Walter Hagen. With a furious slapdash and somewhat agricultural looking golf swing, Hagen did not endear himself to the classicist. But Hagen became a poster boy of golfing irony with an awkward swing and an uncanny ability to negotiate impossible recovery shots to the green and a magical putting touch that bordered on witchcraft. He used his mastery of psychology and showmanship to unnerve and dishevel his opponents by scrambling his way onto the green and making a birdie putt disappear before an incredulous opponent who had properly played down the fairway. Noted British writer A.C.M. Croome captured Hagen's style when he wrote:"He makes more bad shots in a single season than Harry Vardon did from 1890 to 1914, but he beats more immaculate golfers because 'three of those and one of them' counts four and he knows it." Hagen not only looked good but also played well enough, winning four British Open Championships among 11 major titles. He was the first professional to win one million dollars and

to spend two, while espousing his lifelong philosophy, "Never hurry and don't worry. You're here for just a short visit, so don't forget to stop and smell the flowers along the way."

Noted golf architect Alister MacKenzie was commissioned to survey the Old Course at St. Andrews, producing a map in March 1924. During the St. Andrews Open of 1921, MacKenzie first noticed the brash American:

> *I remember, shortly after the war, watching the contestants in the Open Championship or some other important competition playing the 17th at St. Andrews. One of the competitors had pulled his second shot wide of the Road Bunker. I said to the friend who was with me, "Here comes an American. Watch him pitch over the Road Bunker and land in the road beyond." Instead of doing so, he played at a little hillock, only three feet across, to the right of the Road Bunker, and his ball curved in a complete semicircle and lay dead at the pin.*

> *I said to my friend, "That's the best player I have ever seen. Let's follow him to the clubhouse and find out what his name is." We did follow him and we found out his name was Walter Hagen.*

Hagen's brassy style persuaded most observers that seldom if ever did anyone or any course pull the wool over his eyes. One golf writer once cracked, "I wouldn't be surprised if Hagen knows the name of the 'Unknown Soldier'."

THE LUCKY MRS. DEY

Mr. and Mrs. Joe Dey

In the autumn of 1975, Mr. and Mrs. Joe Dey, Jr. were the welcomed guests of the town of St. Andrews and the Royal & Ancient Golf Club who elected Mr. Dey as only the second American Captain. The American couple stayed at the Old Course Hotel adjacent to the Road Hole. The next day at the traditional hangman hour of 8 a.m., Joe Dey drove himself in as Captain in a ceremonial stroke which was timed exactly with the report from a small cannon. Not long thereafter, the field of competitors, members of the Royal & Ancient Golf Club, played over the Old Course in the Autumn Medal.

One of the contestants in the Autumn Medal tournament was also a guest at the Old Course Hotel. When he was not serving as a past chairman of Lloyds of London, Ian Findlay was not infrequently found on his home course in Kent where the Royal St. George's Golf Club is strategically positioned in the "Garden of England." After surveying the Road Hole from his hotel room and contemplating the next day's adventures, Findlay found himself engaged in an animated after-dinner discussion with a charming American lady. Well on in the conversation, Ian learned the identity of the lady to be none other than the wife of the future R&A Captain— Mrs. Joe Dey. "Her husband, she told me, was attending an official dinner with the R&A." After learning that Mr. Findlay was going to be playing in the Autumn Medal, Mrs. Dey ominously announced "Oh, well then, I will come out and watch you." Although an accomplished player in his own right, Mr. Findlay would have preferred to have hidden the light of his talents under a bushel. The burden of displaying his talents to a distinguished audience was a task for which he had not bargained. He gently, but firmly, advised Mrs. Dey that her energies would be well spent on other endeavors. The prospect of having to play up to someone else's expectations cast a daunting shadow on the next day's play.

As one might suspect, Findlay struck off from the first tee and while struggling on the way out, was at least thankful that Mrs. Dey had taken his advice and not borne witness to his travails. However, at the 17th, Ian played his second shot safely onto the green but below the bank which runs around to the front of the green, the ball being to the right of the formidable Road Bunker. While surveying his opportunity beyond the bank toward the center of the green, Ian spied the flag. Beyond the flag, over the green, stood the redoubtable Mrs. Dey! Mr. Findlay and Mrs. Dey exchanged smiles and waves which were borne of nervousness on the part of Mr. Findlay who, unlike Ms. Dey, was well aware of the dangers looming from every quarter. Findlay settled over the ball with his putter and fairly struck his ball which climbed the bank and set off true and straightforward toward the flag, dropping dead center into the hole for a birdie 3! Mrs. Dey clapped her hands together excitedly at the happy but perhaps expected outcome. After briefly mopping his brow, all Mr. Findlay could say was, "I do wish you'd come out earlier, Mrs. Dey!"

BANK ON IT

The wall adjacent to the turnpike road can itself be a formidable hazard, especially when a player finds his ball nestled so closely at the base of the wall that a reasonable stroke cannot be played. Until 1923, the prevailing Local Rules provided that the wall was part of a hazard:

2. *The 17th Hole (Old Course):*

(a) *Along the 17th fairway the grass between the Mussel Road and the wall is part of the hazard.*

(b). *At the 17th green the bank leading down to the gravel footpath is not part of the hazard, but all the rest of the ground between the bank and the wall is part of the hazard.*

On numerous occasions, a player has been compelled to declare his ball unplayable when nestled against the wall. But occasionally a player is able to demonstrate that the ingenuity of a golfer is probably limitless.

In one Walker Cup competition, Francis Ouimet found his ball in such an uncompromising position against the wall. But rather than suffer the ignominy of the penalty, however, Ouimet fashioned a carom shot in which he actually drove the ball into the wall itself, causing the ball to ricochet to within three feet of the hole. Ouimet was successfully able to negotiate the putt, permitting him to halve the hole. He was then required to make three at the home hole to halve his match with Roger Wethered. Ouimet had followed Harry Vardon's tried and tested maxim, "Whatever you do, keep on hitting the ball."

A birdseye view of the Road Hole.

THE SANDS OF NAKAJIMA

Occasionally, the Road Hole has cruelly victimized even the best modern golfer. In the 1978 Open championship, Tsuneyuki "Tommy" Nakajima played himself into reasonable position to vie for the championship on the final day while opening with rounds of 70 and 71. Three months earlier, Nakajima had plumbed the depths of golfing despair when he required an ominous 13 strokes to complete Augusta National's 13th hole at "Amen Corner" during The Masters. When asked whether he had lost his concentration, Tommy guilelessly rejoined, "No. I lost count."

In his third round in the Open, Tommy came to the 17th tee needing two par 4s to finish with another fine 71. He took no chances with his drive, which was positioned properly on the fairway. That was followed by another ostensibly well-played stroke to the front-left of the green. However, seasoned observers would note that this is not the proper place to be. Although there appears to be a 20-foot wide opportunity to putt over the ledge and onto the top tier of the green, actually that is not the case at all. In fact, there is only a three-foot ledge that must be traversed on the right edge of the green if the stroke is to be successful. If the ball has too little speed and does not reach the narrow ledge, the ball will swing around as if gathered by a whirlpool and deposited shamefully in the bottom of the Road Bunker. If the putt is played too strongly it will trickle over the ledge and tumble down onto the treacherous footpath or into the Road beyond. Nakajima suffered the former fate and experienced the ignominy of putting his ball into the Road Bunker. His fourth, fifth, and sixth successive strokes were played with appropriate composure but, on each occasion, the ball returned to the sand from whence it came. Finally, Tommy played a more recklessly exuberant sand stroke and the ball dutifully reached the putting surface for the second time. The pattern of his footprints in the bottom of the bunker told the tale of a calamitous waltz in the desert that cost him a title bid. Two putts later, Tommy recorded a nine. One of the Old Course caddies punctuated the sad event by renaming the bunker "The Sands of Nakajima." When asked for a translation he quipped, "It means 'not enough borrow.'"

Arnold Palmer on the Tom Morris Hole.

WRONG CLUB, CADDIE!

The closest anyone has come to achieving the modern Grand Slam in a single year was Ben Hogan. Sadly, Hogan never played the Road Hole. But in 1953, he won The Masters, the U.S. Open, and the Open Championship at Carnoustie. His legs could not withstand the gauntlet of match play in the PGA, which was the sole major title that eluded him that year.

Hogan's accomplishment was not lost on Arnold Palmer in 1960 when he won The Masters and the U.S. Open Championships. So Palmer traveled to St. Andrews to play in the Centenary Open and test the boundaries of his destiny. Palmer was fortunate to have the advice and counsel of veteran St. Andrews caddie, Jimmy "Tip" Anderson. Like his father before him, Tip became a full-time caddie beginning in 1956. Tip was a native St. Andrean and took up the game at age 15 while soon earning a handicap of four. Partly through the help of his father, Tip acquired an encyclopedic knowledge of the Old Course and the respect of his peers. The Centenary Open initiated a singular caddie-player relationship that endured over 35 years and two British Open Championships in 1961 (Royal Birkdale) and 1962 (Royal Troon). Palmer later "loaned" not only his caddie, Tip, but also his favorite putter to American Tony Lema for the 1964 Open Championship, when Palmer did not play. Tip told Lema where to drive, where to approach, and where to putt. "I always felt I could hit much closer to the traps than Tip recommended," Lema said after he won the championship. "Yet I saw many players hit drives I thought were perfect. They kept finishing in the sand ... Tip Anderson was far more useful to me than anyone can possibly imagine. Without his help, I doubt if I could have won."

During the first three rounds, Palmer listened carefully to the wisdom of his sage caddie. Tip debunked a shibboleth carried over from the hickory shaft era that all drives must be hooked from the tee in order to avoid the bunkers and gorse on the outward nine and the boundary wall on the inward nine. Tip explained that drives which hooked to the left side of the fairway were likely to be either consumed by cavernous bunkers or to be blocked from a clear approach to the green by hillocks or strategically placed green-side bunkers protecting the left. Instead, Tip identified strategic target areas in the middle and right side of the course which would permit the receipt of an approach shot while being unburdened by such obstacles.

Palmer proved to be a good student, as evidenced by his opening rounds of 70, 71, and 70. In the third round, however, a rainstorm rivaling the best Asian monsoon literally swamped the course and required a Saturday finish. Palmer trailed by four strokes from Australian Kel Nagle, and by two from Argentinian Roberto de Vicenzo. Palmer began his epic charge opening with birdies on the first two holes. He went out in 34, matching Nagle's score, and narrowed the gap with a birdie on the 13th and 15th holes. Then the match became a desperately close-run affair when Nagle bogeyed the 15th hole.

That's when Palmer arrived at the Road Hole. During his first three rounds, Arnold had driven perfectly to the fairway, and on each occasion played a number six-iron onto the green. Mysteriously, however, despite Tip's good advice, Palmer three-putted each time for a par. (Since that time, par has been reduced to four.) Desperate not to make the same mistake again, Palmer asked Tip what club he should use. Without hesitation, Tip again recommended a number six-iron: "You know it's a six-iron." Palmer demurred, "Give me my five-iron." As Tip tightened his lips, he declared: "If you take your five-iron, you'll be over in the Road." Palmer was insistent. Whether Palmer was teased into the change of clubs by the softer conditions or simply fortified by his singular bravado, history does not record. But as his caddie surely expected, Palmer's ball bounded over the green, ricocheted off the stone wall and ended in the Road. With gritty determination, Palmer then executed

an exquisite wee putt which hinted at going into the hole, but stayed out. After impassively making his birdie four, Palmer turned to his caddie and scolded: "See there, Tip, what you've been doing? Giving me the wrong club all week!"

Arnold's splendid score of 68 was one more than Kel Nagle, who won that Open. Even now, Palmer has strong feelings about his finish:

Without taking anything at all from Kel Nagle who beat me by one stroke in 1960, I really did think I was going to win, and I felt—and I still feel—that I should have won. But I didn't win and I guess that's just how golf is. Mostly, the fault was in my putting or my inability to read the greens. Tip Anderson may have misread a few, too. We kept seeing breaks—or "borrows" as the Scots called them—that did not exist. And there was the 17th, a hole that I dislike to this day. Mind you, I love the Old Course, but I've never come to terms with the Road Hole, as the 17th has always been known. I keep trying to play it as a par 4 on the card, rather than a par 5, which is more the way it plays. Despite the Road Hole, I've always believed that I would have won the 1960 Open if not for the rain that forced a postponement of the final round until Saturday rather than having two rounds Friday, as was the schedule in those days. I did play well Saturday. My score was 68, but not as well as I would have done against the field, had we played on through Friday afternoon. I felt so strongly that would be my date with destiny that I would have worn out the others. I was fired up, and I just knew I would play that much better than they would.

Joyce Wethered

SHE'S WI'OOT MAIRCY

Perhaps the most distinguished woman golfer who ever swung a club, except Mary Queen of Scots, was Joyce Wethered. Keen observers who watched her play unanimously reported her golfing method was chaste as Grecian statuary. Just before the first leg of the Grand Slam in 1930, Bobby Jones played a friendly foursome match with Joyce Wethered on the Old Course at St. Andrews. Jones' partner, Joyce, played together against Joyce's brother Roger Wethered and Dale Brown, then English Native Amateur Champion. Jones could not believe his eyes, "She did not even half miss one shot, and when we had finished, I could not help saying that I never played with anyone, man or woman, amateur or professional who made me feel so utterly outclassed. I have no hesitancy in saying she is the best golfer I have ever seen." As a Lion in Winter, having watched many decades of the finest golfers in the world, Jones wrote in his autobiography, "The first requisite of a truly sound swing is simplicity. In this respect, I think that Lady Heathcoat-Amory who, as Ms. Joyce Wethered, played superb golf in my day, excels any golfers I have seen. She reduced the matter of hitting the ball to two motions: with one, the club was taken back; with the other, it was swung through. I have found many to agree with me that Ms. Wethered's swing was the most perfect in the world."

Joyce's record supports Jones' extravagant appraisal of her talents. Joyce was English Ladies Champion from 1920 until 1925. She also dominated the British Ladies Championship, winning against formidable competition in 1922, 1924, 1925, and 1929. As a summary to Joyce's astonishing career, it might be recalled that she took part in 12 national championships, Open and English. She won nine of them, was runner-up in two, and a semifinalist in the remaining one. After the exclamation point of her career, in the form of the 1929 British Ladies Title, Joyce joined the Conde Naste staff of writers, and agreed to sell golf equipment for Fortnum and Mason. She was persuaded to tour the U.S. in 1935, and was received with open arms by America.

After Joyce's 1925 British Ladies Championship victory, she retired from the competitive scene for three years. However, when the British Ladies Championship was conducted at St. Andrews in the summer of 1929, Joyce was persuaded to come out of retirement to "repel the American invasion" led by Glenna Collett. Glenna

Collett was no shrinking violet in the world of women's competitive golf either. For two decades, beginning in the 1920s, Glenna was the outstanding player on the American side of the Atlantic. She won an unprecedented six victories in the U.S. Amateur Championship, together with numerous other titles. Only one championship eluded her: the British Ladies Amateur Championship. In 1925, Glenna played against Joyce Wethered for the first time in the British Women's Amateur, contested at Troon. The British spectators enthusiastically supported Joyce. But by the sixth tee, Glenna enjoyed a lead of one-up. That's when Joyce put on a clinic. She scored six birdies, four of them in a row. When the players reached the 11th hole, a steam engine could be seen in the distance, chugging along the tracks parallel to the fairway. The London *Times* reported: "Ms. Wethered holed a long curly putt for a three, characteristically enough with an engine snorting on the line behind her." When asked whether she noticed the train, Joyce responded as if the train was a "lucky portent" for her: "It was puffing smoke in the clouds behind the green in a way that could not very well be ignored. However, I was too well acquainted with the ways of a Scotch engine driver not to know that he was determined to wait to see the hole played to a finish before he continued with his goods to Ayr. Knowing this, there was little to be gained by my waiting. Besides, it was just possible that a train was not an unlucky portent. Whatever may be truth of the supposition, the putt made me three-up and almost decided, I think, the result of the game." At the time she closed out Glenna, four and three, Ms. Wethered was level fours for the match. While Joyce went on to win that championship, Glenna traveled to France, where she won the French Open. But Glenna always longed for another crack at the British Ladies Amateur.

Ms. Collett got her wish in 1929. Unfortunately for Glenna, the result would not be any different than the first occasion they met. The British Press had made a big to-do about the match, and virtually ever man, woman, child, and dog turned out to see it. Glenna got off to a fast start, turning in 34. Ms. Wethered's fans, sensing that Joyce's hopes of victory were going out with the tide, were quaking in their shoes. The venerable Bernard Darwin was suitably impressed with Glenna's play: "She holed some cruel putts, and she did everything well and nothing ill." Joyce only dared to look at Darwin one time. "His dark angular face was black as thunder," she later wrote. Glenna was five-up at the turn. But at the 12th hole, the tide turned. Joyce fought back to two-down by the lunch break. And in the afternoon match,

she stood four-up at the ninth hole. It was an incredible turnaround of nine total holes she won back. By the 15th hole, Ms. Wethered led the match two-up.

The players then came to the "Corner of the Dyke Hole," which is the 16th. The entire right boundary was flanked by the railway line, which ran all the way to the green. The 16th green is tipped slightly toward the railway. Author Douglas Young, in his history, *St. Andrews: Town & Gown, Royal & Ancient*, wrote that as Joyce addressed her putt to win the crucial hole, "A train thundered past ten yards away. When asked why she had not waited for the train to pass first, she asked 'What train?'"

There is no question that Joyce made the famous reply, "What train?" But an issue has been raised about the context. Author Rhonda Glenn, in her book, *Illustrated History of Women's Golf*, says that the episode occurred at Sherringham's 17th green in June 1920 during the English Ladies Closed Amateur Golf Championship, in Joyce's match against defending champion, Cecil Leitch. If it didn't happen at St. Andrews, though, it should have.

One fact is certain. The epic match came to its climax at the Road Hole. Glenna was only able to reach the green with her fourth stroke. The pressure on Joyce to achieve a halve was excruciating. "It's the most trying of all experiences to keep cool just on the brink of winning, and so easy to lose control and spoil it all," Joyce said. "It was a truly wonderful moment. I had wanted this win at St. Andrews so badly, and, with Glenna being such a grand opponent, that match was everything a good match ought to be."

New York Herald Tribune golf writer, Al Laney, worked his way through the throng of spectators, and stood on the road behind the green as Joyce addressed the winning putt that closed out the match, three and one. As Joyce settled over the ball, a man long in the tooth and grizzled in the beard, spoke in a hushed tone, "She's Wi'oot Maircy." Laney added, "Yes, Nae Maircy when the battle was joined but otherwise gentle, unpretentious, and immensely popular."

The 1958 USA World Amateur Team
From left: Billy Joe Patton, Dr. Frank M. Taylor, Jr.,
William Hyndman III, and Charlie Coe.

THE GREATEST SHOT BOBBY JONES EVER SAW

Not long after he returned from Normandy where he landed with Eisenhower's Allied Expeditionary Force on D-Day plus two, Bob Jones was stricken with a rare neurological disease called *syringomyelia*. The disease slowly deteriorated Jones' nervous system and wrecked his once powerful and robust physique. Gradually he was compelled to use one cane, then two, then leg braces, and finally a wheelchair. Through it all, Jones steadfastly and cheerfully refused to focus upon the reversal of his physical plight, saying only, "You have to play the ball as it lies."

After Jones had captured the 1930 Grand Slam, he made what he thought might be his last pilgrimage to Great Britain in 1936 on his way to watch the Berlin Olympic Games. Stopping off for a round at Gleneagles, Jones said he could not bear to be so close to his beloved St. Andrews without a visit. So he dispatched a chauffeur to drive to the Auld Grey Toon and place four names into the ballot box for a tee time including his own, "R.T. Jones, Jr."

The next morning, Jones and his companions traveled to the city to have lunch before their round. As Bob looked out of the window at the Old Course, he noticed several thousand townspeople lining the first fairway and more assembled at the first tee. He was crestfallen. It appeared to him that he had suffered the misfortune of scheduling his match during a major championship.

Little did he know that the news of his arrival had spread like wildfire throughout the town. Virtually the entire town had closed their shops, putting signs in their windows explaining: "Bobby's back." Jones played a magical round, returning a score of level par and reaffirming his status as a beloved hero.

Bob dreamed of his return to Britain after 1936, but never gave it serious consideration until the inaugural 1958 World Team Amateur Championships were announced at the maiden venue of St. Andrews. Bob accepted the duty of Captain for the American Team and for the first time traveled by Pan American Airways across the pond. *"As soon as the world championship was inaugurated I made up my mind that I would make the trip back to St. Andrews. It was a good excuse to come back. Then they made me Captain of the American Team and as soon as that happened I was sure to make the trip."* Only ships had previously transported the Jones entourage on the five previous trips. It was not an uneventful passage, as the fourth engine decided to retire about Gander, Newfoundland, and the

Bill Hyndman and USA Captain Bob Jones.

plane made an unscheduled stop for repairs. The party arrived a full eight hours behind schedule at Prestwick (on October 3) and all but Bob and his wife, name-sake son, and daughter Mary Ellen postponed the immediate continuation to St. Andrews. *"I could not hold off any longer,"* remarked Jones. *"It was a very tiring trip and an eventful one. And as you know my mobility and endurance are less now than they once were."* In his beginning and his end, Bob's health would be the weakest part of his game. Bob joked that the 1958 journey to St. Andrews for the World Amateur Team Championships was negotiated by *"auto, wheelchair, plane— but no donkeys."*

A handful of St. Andreans waited the entire day to greet Jones. Among them was Tom Law, of Angus, who witnessed Bob's magic at St. Andrews in 1930. He greeted Jones as he coursed his way with the aid of two canes from the car to Rusacks Hotel facing the 18th green. *"It's been a long time getting back—22 years. But it's worth waiting for,"* Jones told Jimmy Innes and Alec Robertson, who caddied during several of Bob's Roaring Twenties championships. In the Scottish gloaming on the links, Jones quipped, *"I'm going to get in my electric buggy and travel all over the Old*

Course. It will be the first buggy ever to go round there and I bet you it'll be the last." Bob's words were never so accurate, as no buggies are permitted to this day.

During these matches, Jones' buggy would be much observed and served as the vehicle to unite and reunite many friends and friendships. Bob was joined on the second fairway by Laurie B. Ayton, the 73-year-old native St. Andrean who ably served as golf professional at Evanston C.C. in Illinois. Laurie observed, *"It was a very pleasant meeting. Last time we played together was at St. Petersburg, Florida. On that occasion Bobby had two 69s."* They chatted over old times while traveling in Bob's chariot.

Bob gave several interviews for Henry Longhurst, Arthur Montford and others, including a rookie reporter for the *Dundee Courier*. Bob observed that the general standard of golf had improved "with the steel shafts" being responsible in no small part.

In this contest, the Americans would not prevail over the Australian champions. Nevertheless, the American team would demonstrate a gutty determination not to give the Eisenhower Cup away without a fight. The team had been counseled by Jones not to gamble for the flag on the approach to the treacherous Road Hole. Armed with this admonition, Bill Hyndman III came to the 17th needing 3-4 to tie the Australian team. Jones watched the action from his cart:

> *After a beautiful drive at 17, while waiting for his companions to play their seconds, Bill was pacing up and down like a man possessed. I had the night before told our team to take no chance with the road at 17 unless the situation appeared to be dire. Of course, it was obvious to Bill that if ever a dire situation existed it was now.*

Hyndman surveyed his ball one last time. Then, he looked over to where Jones was sitting in his cart. With his steel blue-grey eyes peering from underneath his felt hat, Jones answered the question with a quick nod of his head. He didn't have to speak a word. His gesture alone empowered Hyndman as if to say, *"Yes, Bill. Go for it!"*

Bill hit his four-iron crisply and the ball arched high over the leaden sky. Soon the onlookers could judge for themselves that the shot was not just a good one. It was nearly perfect, almost holing out and settling possibly five feet from the hole. Down went the eagle putt. Momentum to America. On the home hole, Bill had a fifteen-footer to win. But it would have been foolhardy to three-putt. So, Hyndman coaxed in his par on the home hole and upon the wings of his daring bravado, a play-off was achieved with Australia.

Although the Americans lost the eventual playoff, they acquitted themselves admirably in the process. The drama provided on the closing holes contributed mightily to the popularity of the world matches which continue to this day.

After the matches were completed, Bob Jones wrote a letter to John Ames, then USGA President, reporting his impressions of the Old Course, the tournament, and the stroke which he called "truly one of the greatest shots I have ever seen." The Philadelphia Golfers Association also honored Hyndman with a photograph of the Road Hole and a brass plate commemorating the famous stroke.

If anyone could be trusted to give an accurate appraisal of what constitutes a great shot, that man would surely be Bobby Jones.

The letter sent by Jones to Ames dated October 16, 1958 is of such significant historical value that it is reproduced herewith:

Mr. John D. Ames, President　　　　　　　　　　　　　　　*October 16, 1958*
United States Golf Association
135 LaSalle Street
Chicago 3, Illinois

Dear John:

I know that such is not expected of me, but I must give myself the pleasure of making to you and the Executive Committee of the USGA a report upon the performance at St. Andrews in the World Cup competition of the splendid American team of which I had the honor to be the Captain.

The result is, of course, well known. Yet, even though the victory was not ours, the achievement of second place represented a considerable triumph attributable mainly to the highest qualities of character and perseverance on the part of our team.

It is surely obvious that a non-playing captain can do very little to influence the result of any golf team match. In the World Cup competition in its present form, there is absolutely nothing for the captain to do, because the selection of his players and the scores to be counted is a matter of routine decided solely upon the scores accomplished. I had thought that the intimate and thorough knowledge of the Old Course at St. Andrews, which I am sure I possess, might be

of some value to the players. As it turned out, I found that although I know St. Andrews in the spring, I had no useful knowledge of the course and playing conditions that existed in October. With the wet ground and high winds, the course was playing extremely long and all the subtleties I had come to know and respect had vanished. I needed only one round with our team members to be convinced that there was no contribution I could make along this line.

I must confess that this discovery came as quite a shock to me, but I must proudly say at the same time that it influenced my team members not a bit, because they were ever eager for my consultation and advice.

The only aspect of the play which I felt that I might influence to any degree involved the well rooted conviction on my part that the decisive factor was going to be the relative ability of the various players to stand up to the enormous psychological pressure bound to be exerted by this great golf course under these conditions. About all that I could do was to try to make certain that each of our men should always realize that others were being subjected to the same pressures. I know from experience how easy it is to forget that the wind is blowing on all alike and that others, too, are having to call upon their ultimate resources in order to stand up under the buffetings of a tremendous test.

Under all these circumstances, the highest tribute that could be paid to our players is the simple statement that not one of them in six rounds of competition ever played one careless shot or for one instant relaxed his vigilance. More than once, I am sure, they wanted to escape from the unrelenting strain, but never did they yield to the temptation.

The finish on Saturday, by which our team gained a tie with Australia, was one of the most dramatic imaginable. I am sure you are aware that the method of scoring made it very difficult to ascertain at all times the precise state of the contest. You may be interested to learn just how the thrilling events of Saturday afternoon were unfolded to this observer.

Bill Hyndman of our team was playing in the last threesome with Wolstenholme of Great Britain and McDougall of New Zealand. As I dashed about the course on my electric buggy, the varying bits of intelligence available to me soon indicated that our cause was in a very bad way, according to scoreboards. The Australians and New Zealanders had done quite well on the outward nine, whereas we had not. The British, too, had turned for home with a lead of a

couple of strokes over us.

An interesting sidelight might be that in a close finish of this kind, none of the rival captains were trying to do any "Master-minding" or to confuse or to conceal information from their opposite numbers. Indeed, I was in free communication with and got a good deal of information from Gerald Micklem, the British captain, and Jim Schouler of the New Zealand team. I had sat within a few yards of Micklem as his man Perowne holed a birdie three at the sixteenth and later it was from him and Pat Ward-Thomas of the Manchester Guardian that I learned the exact state of the game as Bill Hyndman was putting for three at the seventeenth.

At last arriving behind the sixteenth green in much excitement, I saw Hyndman play a lovely second shot six feet to the right of the hole, with his British and New Zealand companions both over-playing. At this point, I did not know the penalty of two strokes for striking the flag incurred by Bob Stevens of Australia on the tenth hole, nor did I know of the misfortune of Peter Toogood of the same team on the seventeenth. As I watched Hyndman prepare to putt for his three at sixteen, it was my appraisal that if he could make this putt, he might conceivably finish in 4 - 3 for 71, which might, by an equal stretch of the imagination, give us a tie with Great Britain for second, or even a clear second. There seemed no hope of catching the Australians. But Bill missed the putt.

Upon seeing me in my buggy, Hyndman came over to ask about the situation. The best that I could tell him was, as I have said, and that I thought he should go for a 4 - 3 finish, never dreaming that a three at seventeen was at all possible. After a beautiful drive at seventeen, while waiting for his companions to play their second Bill was pacing up and down like a man possessed. I had the night before cautioned our team to take no chances with the road at seventeen unless the situation appeared to be dire. Of course, it was obvious to Bill, as it was to me, that if ever a dire situation existed, it was now. I think he had completely made up his mind to go for broke on this hole, but he must have wanted some sort of release from me. As he paced up and down behind his ball, he said, as much to himself as to me, "Well, I guess I had better go for it, Bobby." And I replied, "Yes, I guess you had."

That second shot with a four iron was truly one of the greatest shots I have

ever seen. I actually thought the ball was going to hole out. That did it, and as we learned in a few moments, Hyndman needed only to par the last hole, which he did, to give us a tie with Australia, and Wolstenholme, having required five at seventeen, likewise finished with a par to leave the British one stroke behind.

I think our team lost on the putting greens. Charlie Coe, wherever I saw him, was hitting the ball beautifully. Even on the greens, and again, he barely missed from short range. Hyndman was always swinging quite well. But he, too, had putting troubles from the very moment he stepped onto the course in practice. Patton, though he worked with a fervor and determination I have never seen surpassed, did not really strike his true playing form until the play-off round, but he, too, nullified brilliant play from tee to green by some unaccountable putting lapses. Taylor was in full possession of his usual immaculate game from tee to green, insofar as the elements and gigantic golf course would permit, but he did suffer from a bursitis-type ailment to his left shoulder and from badly blistered heels as a result of having his golf shoes misplaced along with his clubs on the trip over. Bud was never able to summon the extra slashing power so necessary to the playing of this kind of golf course under these conditions.

Above all, it was more than gratifying to have so many people say to me, just as though I had had anything to do with it, that my American players were so completely charming. Although all the boys did everything in their power to win, they realized, as everyone at St. Andrews did, that there were aspects of the competition far more important than winning. None of us are naive enough to expect that a golf tournament will accomplish miracles, but I know that many seeds of international friendship were sown on the Old Course. Perhaps we may dare to hope that some lasting good may result. For me, my association with Charlie, Bill, Billy Joe and their wives, and with Bud Taylor, was one which I shall always remember with an enormous amount of pride and pleasure.

Most sincerely,

Robert T. Jones, Jr.
RTJ:jam

79

Watts Gunn and Roland MacKenzie

DESPERATE TIMES CALL FOR DESPERATE MEASURES

It is not surprising that the pivotal hole in the 1926 Walker Cup Matches proved to be the Road Hole. But it is astonishing that the margin of victory hung in the balance of a match played by a 19-year-old lad from suburban Washington, D.C. named Roland MacKenzie. At 6 foot 2 and 185 pounds, Roland was quite an American secret weapon. He was fourth in the long-driving contest at Royal Lytham & St. Anne's in 1926 before the Open with a poke of 267 yards. And Roland was a seasoned amateur player well beyond his chronological age. He played on the 1926, 1928, and 1930 Walker Cup teams for America.

The tension of the 1926 matches was so dense it could be cut with a knife. Perhaps the crucial match that sounded the funeral dirge for Great Britain was between American Captain Bob Gardner and Roland MacKenzie versus Honorable W.G.E. Brownlow (Lord Lurgan) and Edward F. Eustace Storey. The players came to the Road Hole after a brave comeback achieved by Brownlow and Storey to square the match. The British team appeared to have taken the momentum and played two splendid strokes to the front of the green. The Americans, on the other hand, played like drunken sailors. Roland hit a wild-hooking tee shot all the way across the second hole and nearly into the whins bordering its fairway. Captain Gardner did little to instill confidence in his youthful partner. He cold shanked a brassie that did a rapid duck and drake right across the fairway into horridly rough grass only five or six yards short of the Road. The American's ball was fully 70 yards from the green. Fortunately, the ball was found by a member of the R&A standing nearby. Roland could hardly see the top of the ball where it lay. The only stroke available to the young man was a desperate slashing chop downward onto the ball. British Captain Robert Harris watched in amazement at what happened next:

MacKenzie extricated it in the only possible way—he hit it bang on the head, it bounced in the air, the ball following on after and above the clubhead, reached the course first bounce and with the spin imparted by the top it trundled onto the green.

Gardner then nonchalantly walked over to the ball to putt it into the hole as if to convey the absurd notion that his team had planned these pyrotechnics all along. Bernard Darwin could only shake his head in disbelief as the Americans rubbed it in:

These things will happen but that was an astonishing piece of luck, admittedly taken noble advantage of, is undeniable.

Roland then sealed the win with a 20-foot putt on the home hole after Gardner made another extraordinary chip from the steep bank behind the green.

British Captain Harris felt as though he had been twice bitten by a snake. In the last contest at St. Andrews in 1923, he previously met Captain Gardner under similar circumstances. Their singles match came to the home hole all square. Gardner topped his tee shot which almost squirted into the Swilken Burn. He followed that with a second topped stroke using a brassie that hopped like a hare all the way to the green and darted into the rough grass on the bank. Apparently unperturbed, the unflappable Gardner next gently extricated the ball with his niblick and it ran down 10 inches from the hole. He made that putt to halve the hole and win by one-up. Ho-hum.

Twenty-five years later, when the two players regathered together, Robert Harris teased Gardner, *"Tell us about your three topped shots at the last hole in the 1923 Walker Cup singles."* Gardner simply replied, *"Now, Bob, you know I always play these shots that way at this hole."*

NO RESPECTER OF PERSONS

The Road Hole has proved to be no respecter of persons. Even golfers with the finest competitive pedigree are not exempt from its challenges. An important example is the accomplished American amateur, Chick Evans. Evans was the first person to win "The Double," comprising the U.S. Amateur and U.S. Open in the same year—1916. Evans also won four straight Western Amateur Championships, which were considered major titles. He annexed a second U.S. Amateur title in 1920.

In 1911 Evans traveled to Prestwick during his campaign for the British Amateur Championship, and subsequently to play in the French Amateur Championship, which he won. After Harold Hilton had captured the Amateur title, Evans decided to try his hand at the home of golf. "To play one round on the historic course had been my real reason for crossing the Atlantic. I played not one, but several rounds on the course. A temporary membership and friendly treatment made my Scottish journey ever memorable."

In his first confrontation with the Road Hole, however, Evans could not avoid the peril of his ball going onto the Road. In his only visit to St. Andrews, Evans was made a believer. The Road Hole is indeed the toughest in the world. Evans discovered later that he might have had an easier time on the Road Hole if he hadn't been "straight-jacketed" by his attire. It seems that one of his friends, USGA President Silas H. Strawn, bought Chick a new tweed waist coat and suit, thinking that the weather might be cold and nasty in Great Britain. Chick was pretty excited about joining the likes of Vardon, Ray, and Taylor by wearing his coat. But the weather turned unseasonably warm. Chick desperately wanted to remove his coat because he was sweating profusely. But there was one catch—he didn't have a belt for his trousers. He toughed it out and played the entire match until the final hole, which was halved. On the first play-off hole, Chick's ball found a bunker, and it was obvious to him that his cause was lost. So he finally took off the "coat of torture," which provided "great relief, however unproductive."

Arthur Montford interviewing Bob Jones at St. Andrews in 1958.

THE GREATEST STROKE THAT NEVER MATTERED

By Arthur Montford

The crowds which flocked into the Old Grey Town for the last round of the 1970 Open Championship soon headed for their favorite spots. Some would be on the move all day as the battle unfolded, seat-sticks in one hand, provisions in the other. The most popular vantage point of all, as always, was soon filled to capacity— the "bleachers" overlooking the famous 17th green. The early starters had not yet moved into view, but the atmosphere was one of anticipation. At this hole, the destiny of the Championship could easily be settled.

It promised to be a day of wonderful cut and thrust, but the fresh breeze coming off the Eden estuary and blowing left-to-right across the course suggested that the fine scoring of the first two days would not be repeated.

Any one of six or seven competitors stood on the first tee knowing that a score of par (72) or just under could do it. Lee Trevino, on 208, led by two from Tony Jacklin, Doug Sanders, and Jack Nicklaus. Peter Oosterhuis and Neil Coles were one shot behind, and Harold Henning was at 212.

As the story of the day unraveled, Lee Trevino fell out of the running with a 77, and the English trio of Jacklin, Oosterhuis, and Coles all shot 76.

Henning could do no better than 73 for 285, which left Nicklaus and Sanders center stage. Both played resolutely, Nicklaus in the game in front of Sanders. At the turn, Nicklaus led by a shot, 35 to 36 —admirable scoring in the freshening breeze— only to give the shot back at the 11th, and when Nicklaus dropped a stroke at the par-4 16th, Sanders was at last in front. Two fours would win him the Open. But as Sanders recalled from his Houston base 30 years later, he thought he had given it away at the 17th:

My drive was good. I had driven beautifully all week, in fact. The choice for the second shot was never in doubt: a four-iron aimed for the bottom right-hand side of the green with a slight right to left shape to draw on to the green, not far enough to be threatened by the Road. However, I didn't get a good bounce and, to be honest, slightly underestimated the strength of the wind, both factors combining to drag the ball into the Road Bunker short left. It was then, and still is in my view, the toughest bunker in the world.

Contrary to what has often been reported before, I DIDN'T play my sand wedge, preferring instead my pitching wedge for the extra power I knew it would give me down through the sand and under the ball. It was simply the best bunker shot I'd ever played, finishing just two feet from the pin with a straight knock-in for my four. The applause from the spectators just a few yards away was very, very moving. They must have thought that with a four at the last to win, I was within touching distance of the claret jug.

Alas, there isn't much to say about what happened next. My final drive was perfect, aimed on the clubhouse clock. I then had 76 yards to the pin, but with the adrenalin pumping I simply hit the ball too far over the Valley of Sin. I putted down four feet short, but didn't even hit the hole with the left-to-right putt that would have won me the Open.

Tied with Big Jack, we replayed 18 holes the next day. It was close but I have to say I never really felt I was going to win it. We were level after 17 holes but Jack, after taking off his sweater, as everyone knows, put his ball past the pin at the 324 yard 18th, and although I got my four this time—of course!—he chipped to six feet and holed out for a three and a 72 to my 73.*

I never got this close to a 'major' again, and I suppose that if I HAD won the Open, my bunker shot at the 17th would have been hailed as one of the great Championship-winning shots of all time. Even now, though, everyone still wants to ask me about my three putts at the last hole! That's golfers for you!

*The only player to beat par on the final day with a 71 was John Panton, now Honorary Professional of the R&A. He was 53 years of age at the time and tied ninth with Peter Thomson.

THE MOST DASTARDLY STROKE
EVER PERPETRATED
AT THE ROAD HOLE

As one might imagine, in the two-thousand-year history of St. Andrews, there have been myriad wonderful demonstrations of courtesy and consideration exchanged between its citizens and visitors. And it continues to this day.

But the darkest day, and the most dastardly act ever visited off the course was in 1528 when theology professor Patrick Hamilton was accused of heresy. It seems that Patrick had been traveling over the lands of Europe, and had met a theologian in Wittenberg, Germany named Martin Luther. Luther persuaded Patrick that people were saved by grace through belief in Jesus Christ rather than belief in witches and toad frogs. So Patrick expatriated this notion to Scotland along with a singular resolve to evangelize the golfers and town folk.

As a member of the University faculty, Patrick should have realized that he was making waves with his new theology. In fact, he knew it. Archbishop Beaton of Glasgow was the fellow who passed out the orders in those days. He had a problem with Patrick's teachings. Beaton's "conscience clattered" over the notion preached by Patrick that a "good man does good deeds." But it doesn't work the other way around. Just because a man does good deeds, it doesn't mean he is a saved man. It sounds like an issue that families are warned to avoid like the plague during reunions and holiday gatherings. That's what Archbishop Beaton thought, too. He got a sandspur in his saddle over the subject, and decided that St. Andrews would be a better place if Patrick had his right to live revoked. So Patrick was led to the gateway of St. Salvators at high noon, and a fire was built. Only the fellows who built the fire must have been golfers and not boy scouts. Because the fire wasn't designed to achieve a quick resolution of the death sentence. Those gentle readers who are opposed to the death penalty might want to skip to the next paragraph. Since the chief eyewitness said that Patrick was "roasted rather than burned from noon until six o'clock at night." The executioners were so derelict in their duties that Patrick finally held up his scorched hands and beseeched his tormentors crying out, "Have ye no dry wood and gunpowder?" Patrick could have fled with the help of his brother who was a sheriff. But he chose to die like a hero for his beliefs, and was thus the first martyr of the Scottish Reformation. Even today, his ini-

Vinny Giles' perfect stroke.

tials "PH" are set in stone in the sidewalk at the gateway of St. Salvadors Tower on North Market Street.

Thankfully, social convention on the Old Course has never deteriorated to the depths of Patrick Hamilton's martyrdom. However, there is one episode which shall go down in the annals of infamy in Walker Cup history dubbed "The Most Dastardly Stroke Ever Played." That was the occasion on which Sir Michael Bonallack met Vinny Giles in the singles matches. Sir Michael is no stranger to links competition. He won the British Amateur championship on five occasions. But he didn't close his trophy case after that. Instead, he won five English Amateur titles, played nine times in the Walker Cup competitions, played six times for the Eisenhower Trophy, and won or tied four times in the English Strokeplay Championship. For you Hogan fans, Sir Michael exhibited his skills for Ben Hogan in a 1966 Masters appearance together.

Sir Michael's competition in the Walker Cup, Marvin "Vinny" Giles, was also a grizzled veteran. Giles won the U.S. Amateur in 1972, thrice finished second, and added the British Amateur in 1975 at Hoylake. He won 70% of his 15 Walker Cup matches.

These two titans of Amateur golf were level standing on the 17th tee. Both hit reasonable drives over the black sheds. Sir Michael then played his approach just past the Road Bunker. The spectators must have seen him licking his chops as Giles hit his approach with a wee too much draw. It landed, bobbled, and jostled along the small swales until it terminated its journey on a small brae just to the side of the Road Bunker. Vinny would be presented with perhaps the most terrifying proposition in the short game. He would be required to softly loft his ball over the steep wall of the Road Bunker, land it with sufficient spin to reduce its velocity on the downsloping green, and pray that it would not go into the Road. A crude analogy to the degree of difficulty would be landing a Boeing 757 jumbo jet with full reverse thrusters down a children's slide, and hoping it didn't ooze off the end of the runway. After all, Sir Michael's broadsword was poised for victory.

If anyone can execute such a persnickety athletic challenge as this, it is Vinny Giles. "I hit that little pitch shot over the bunker, and it trickled along the downslope of the green and teetered on the edge and about half a second later it toppled into the cinders on the Road!" says Vinny, when he describes the shot today from the warmth of his Virginia offices. Sir Michael then struck while the iron was hot, putting up the back of the green and down within three feet from victory. Then he

confidently leaned on his putter near the collar of the green as he observed Giles' next stroke. Sir Michael was entitled to wear the smile of the Cheshire cat, and, except for his innate and genuine modesty, he might well have done so.

Giles ambled down onto the cinder-laden road armed to the teeth with his faithful sandwedge. The character of the Road would dictate this stroke. In those days, the cinders were loose and the consistency of the roadway was uncertain.

"I tried to play a splashing shot like hitting 'oot of a sand bunker," Giles says about the next shot. "But I caught the equator of the ball with the leading edge of the club. It came 'oot of there pretty hot." To say that the ball came 'oot pretty hot is no understatement. "It hit the round metal flagstick over halfway up from the hole: Bang! And then it dropped like a stone into the hole. A dastardly stroke, indeed. That's four for Giles. After that who could blame Sir Michael for missing his tying putt? Not his teammates, who prevailed the next day in spite of being two behind after the first day of competition. It was their second consecutive Walker Cup victory at St. Andrews, the first being celebrated in 1938.

Sir Michael and Vinny were reunited the following spring at the traditional amateur dinner preceding The Masters Tournament in Augusta. As they sat down to dinner, R&A Secretary Keith MacKenzie walked into the room carrying the very flagstick that conspired with Giles in that Walker Cup match with Sir Michael. He presented it to Vinny and today it is the only golf object hanging on the walls of Vinny's Virginia abode. Suffice it to say that if Vinny's rocket shot had not struck the flagstick, the ball would have arrived in Augusta long before he did.

VICTORY WITHOUT A
SINGLE SHOT FIRED

(Strath vs. Martin - 1876)

Those who know about such things report that it is difficult enough to win a championship without suffering from the hands of a committee decision on a controversial interpretation of the rules governing golf. Bob Jones made a poignant observation when he said, "If you enter a tournament and don't cheat, and happen to make the lowest score, they have to give you the cup." In theory, it sounds simple enough. But try putting that maxim into practice, as for example, on the occasion in 1957 when Bobby Locke was two putts away from victory on the home hole. Bobby putted close to the hole and marked his ball. Locke's playing partner then asked dear old Bobby if he would be kind enough to move his marker off his intended line to the hole. Locke obliged. But he forgot to replace his marker in its original position two putter-head lengths from where it lay. Instead, Bobby replaced his ball directly in front of his marker, and in front of many thousands of viewers on the telly, he made the putative winning putt. But someone watching on the telly told on Locke. And the R&A Championship Committee took the matter under advisement. Locke had a lot going in his favor. He undisputedly had four feet from the hole with three strokes to spare from his challenger Peter Thomson. The championship was concluded. And wearing his outfit consisting of white plus fours, shirt and tie and oatmeal cap, Locke could have been mistaken for the *archbishop's butler if not the archbishop himself* according to venerable Henry Longhurst. The Committee invoked the rule of equity which requires judgments to be made with the *spirit of the game* in mind. It could not be earnestly contended that it was fair and just to take the title from a man who was four feet from the object of his desires with three strokes to spare and had not enhanced his own position by failing to replace his marker two putter lengths from whence it was. So Locke got his prompt favorable ruling and his coveted trophy.

But happy outcomes like this don't just happen to everyone. Take, for instance, the controversy surrounding the erroneous scorecard incident involving 1968 Masters contender Roberto deVincenzo. The rule of equity isn't for everybody. And one must always remember that golf is a singular game wherein the player must police his own conduct, announce rules infractions voluntarily, and play all his foul

The Famous Road Hole.

balls where they may lie. In short, a golfer must endure the *rub of the green* whether sweet or sour.

It was more the latter for Davie Strath in the 1876 Open championship. Davie's brother, Andrew, had already won the 1865 Open at Prestwick. And it was his turn to be the favorite to win this one. Davie had finished four times in the top five spots of the Open. He didn't help his cause in the first round when he missed a two-inch putt at the 15th hole. He was tied with Bob Martin. But by the 14th hole on the second and final round, Strath must have started to feel the pressure.

Spectators had no crowd control measures in those days and everyone scurried to get a good vantage point. Now, there is an ancient rule of golf and etiquette stating essentially that no player should play his stroke until the players in front are out of range. In the excellent treatise on *Challenges and Champions* by Behrend and Lewis, this Rule 2 of the Royal and Ancient 1875 Code was stated as follows:

> *When two parties meet on the putting green, the party first there may claim the privilege of holing out and any party coming up must wait until the other party has played out the hole and on no account play the balls up less they should annoy the parties who are putting.*

As he stood on the fairway waiting to play his approach to the 14th green, Davie knew the rule well. He elected to play his stroke for whatever reason while the group ahead was still on the green and putting out. Davie cracked a good one all right. It was so good, he hit St. Andrews upholsterer Mr. Hutton square on the forehead. Mr. Hutton was felled like a giant redwood by that blow. If Davie intended to gain an advantage, the plan failed as he made 6 on that hole and the 15th as well. Strath thus came to the Road Hole needing 10 strokes on the last two holes to win.

By the time Davie played his third stroke to the Road Hole, hundreds of St. Andreans had heard of his adventure and possibility of winning the championship at last. He was not an unpopular contestant. But he got himself in a cauldron of hot controversy on the approach shot. Because the folks on the green had not quite finished their business when he let the iron stroke fly, helped by the tailwind to the green, he got the daily double — that is, for the second time in four holes, Davie's ball struck a player on the green ahead. This time, he was lucky that the ball did not go into the Road as plenty of spectators said would have happened but for the fortuitous ricochet. Davie made 5 there. And he made 6 at the last hole to tie Bob Martin.

Ordinarily, a play-off would have settled the tie on the next Monday. But some diligent philosophical prisoner of the rules lodged a complaint. Strath was accused of intentionally gaining an advantage by using the wall of spectators as a shield to protect him from the wrath of the Road on 17. His intent was to be inferred from the fact that he previously felled Mr. Hutton on the 14th hole. And, thereafter, he repeated the foul on 17. *Falsus in uno falsus in ominibus.*

As the case was presented to the Council of the R&A, the defense of selective enforcement of the rules was raised on Davie's behalf. Strath was not the only one to strike a spectator during the competition, and therefore, he should not be singled out for disparate punishment while other guilty offenders should go free. According to historian Bobby Burnet in his able history of *The St. Andrews Opens*, the matter was further complicated by the additional charge that Strath's caddy had not recorded the scores properly on the official R&A scorecard given to the contestants.

With so much to ponder, the council ordered the play-off to ensue on Monday. Both the course and the Council apparently rested on Sunday and no decision was rendered. Besides, there were five other players involved in the Monday play-offs for 4th, 5th, 6th, 8th, and 9th places. Might as well have the championship play-off and see what happens.

When Monday came, the other matches went out as planned. But the Council hadn't decided Strath's fate yet. Strath didn't think that was fair to delay the decision and force him to play under the cloud of protest. So he decided to do nothing. In this contest of strong wills, the Council of the R&A would prove omnipotent if not omniscient.

As for Bob Martin, the die was cast. He showed up for the dance but found no willing partner. So, he took one of the most carefree Sunday strolls in history around the Old Course by himself and his well-wishers. And when he returned, he was declared champion and awarded the £10 first prize and the trophy. Strath never was disqualified since his case was rendered moot by the fact that he never won the play-off. He was awarded second place and the £5 prize.

Oh, yes. Mr. Hutton, who was felled at the 14th, recovered nicely and was able to walk home. He returned to his upholstery business and probably lectured fellow golfers on the virtues of yelling *Fore*.

As for the *spirit of the game*, well, you'll have to ask Bobby Locke about that. You can probably guess what Davie Strath's opinion is. And Roberto de Vicenzo, too.

ALL'S FAIR

Despite its overriding popularity due in part to its historicity, the Road Hole has its fair share of critics. Few are bold enough to subject their opinions to peer review. Put simply, they fear the retribution of being labeled a heretic for criticizing the Old Course. When a Master, like Van Gogh, first exhibited his works during his lifetime, it was easy for the critics to howl. Several centuries later, after the majority of reputable art critics have universally acclaimed his paintings as masterpieces, a naysayer is more likely to be cast out of the fold, shunned and avoided. So it is with the Road Hole. Some decry its penal nature and the fact that bad shots are sometimes rewarded, and good shots are sometimes cruelly punished. Others celebrate its strategic virtues and the endless variety of ways that are presented to play it.

Perhaps it should be remembered that golf is a sport and not a game. *Golf enables us to advance in the great business of being a human being. The man who regards golf as a matter of "card and pencil" is not a golfer at all, for he has lost his soul in arithmetic, whereas the true golfer puts his soul into the game for the love of it, and not because it amounts to a mere matter of mathematics as he wends his way back to the clubhouse,* wrote University of London Psychology Professor Henry Chellew.

There is a good answer to those misguided souls who bitterly criticize the Road Hole and the Old Course as penal and unfair. The genius of the Road Hole and its brethren is variety. Whoever said "variety is the spice of life" was talking about the Road Hole. The truth is that there are an infinite number of ways to play the Road Hole. That is why Bobby Jones said hundreds of times that he liked the Old Course better than any golf course he had ever played, and although he had played it many, many times, its charm for him increased with every round.

When he was asked to contrast the golf required to play the Old Course at St. Andrews and to play on the best American courses, Jones replied, *I have found that most of our courses may be played correctly the same way round after round.*

The way we build a course in this country, the fellow who designs it tells you how you must play it. He gives you a fairway and a green and some bunkers around it, and he tells you you've got to drive here. If you don't you're in the woods or some other place. St. Andrews, you can drive almost anywhere, but if you haven't picked the right spot according to the weather conditions and the conditions of the ground, you're at a disadvantage.

I didn't like St. Andrews at all when I first played it...But pretty soon I studied the course, and by the time I played there in '27, and again in '30, I felt that I knew it.

Jones saw plenty of American courses that employed the "penal" philosophy, using rough bunkers and hazards. These courses provided no options. There was only one safe place to put the tee ball, and since the only obvious choice was to avoid the trouble, no thought was needed or appreciated. The approach shot also left the player with little choice. The green was usually overwatered and sloped up toward the back, so there was little chance the ball would go over if it hit the green. No spin on the ball was required. This type of course tended to promote and reward a mechanical player whose skill level was focused solely on pursuing the straight and obvious route. Jones and a few other thinking-people believed that this "rote" type of mechanical game robbed golf of all mystery, romance, and adventure because it did not require the player to use the sometimes valuable six inches between the ears. Nor did it encourage the player to exercise his judgment in the face of the varying conditions of wind, rain, or dry ground. The correct placement of each shot should be rewarded. But length without control ought to be punished.

The first American Amateur Champion was Charles Blair Macdonald who learned his golf under the tutelage of Old Tom Morris at the Old Course at St. Andrews. Macdonald had something important to say about people who whine and complain about golf courses and golf holes that they think are too difficult:

So many people preach equity in golf. Nothing is so foreign to the truth. Does any human being receive what he conceives as equity in his life? He has got to take the bitter with the sweet, and as he forges through all the intricacies and inequalities which life presents, he proves his metal. In golf the cardinal rules are arbitrary and not founded on eternal justice. Equity has nothing to do with the game itself. If founded on eternal justice the game would be deadly dull to watch or play. The essence of the game is inequality, as it is in humanity. The conditions which are meted out to the players, such as inequality of the ground, cannot be governed by a green committee with the flying divots of the players or their footprints in the bunkers. Take your medicine where you find it and don't cry. Remember that the other fellow has got to meet exactly the same inequalities.

In considering the fairness of the Old Course—and the Road Hole in particular—we might also derive some benefit in understanding the very reason for playing golf in the first instance. Professor Chellew makes a good argument that golf "makes tired men renew their energies, bored men become interested, old men become young again, young men become philosophers, philosophers become human, and live close to the heart of things—nature."

A good number of St. Andreans have already picked up on this point. And Robert Browning in his *A History of Golf* has traveled an admirable distance to expatriate these notions to those who live on the west side of the Atlantic Ocean:

At the beginning of the century, as the late Lord Birkenhead wrote in his book "America Revisited," published soon after the First World War, the average American man of business 'was conceived of, and not altogether with injustice, as one who left home early and returned late, employing the long day in the feverish interests of Wall Street; he became dyspeptic at forty, and he very often died at fifty. In the interval (if he were successful), he accumulated a vast fortune. His wife and his beautiful daughters enjoyed it; but as far as he was concerned the rare alleviations of a hectic life coincided with a few hurried visits to Europe.' But golf, Lord Birkenhead declared, has changed all this and has taught even the hustlers 'to realize that life is short, health vital, dollars incapable of transfer to the next world, and that therefore there is much to be said for a reasonable enjoyment of life in this.'

The essence of golf at St. Andrews and the Old Course is variety which produces adventure. The added spices of luck and the companionship of congenial friends, fully add to the mix and promote a zest for life that no other activity can provide. Well, maybe except for one, and that is not work. But that is yet another subject.

As you will see from the episodes contained in this work, no one is alone in the joys and frustrations presented in playing the Road Hole. It has been attacked in vain and in glory by the mighty professional and the lowly amateur over these many years. It has continued to provide unbridled enjoyment to everyone who faces its challenges. I can't wait to have another crack at the Road Hole on my next visit to St. Andrews. Or, for that matter, let it have another crack at me.

Old Tom Morris surveying his Old Course.

THE BRIDGE HOLE

St. Andrews Links has been celebrated for many virtues other than its antiquity: the artful location of its bunkers, the prevalence of strategic banks and braes, and its plateau putting greens which taunt the player with a choice between approaching by putter or lofting stroke. But the Old Course has another astonishing attribute. It can be played with equal enjoyment from a right-a or left-hand routing scheme of its holes. It is, in a sense, "reversible."

From earliest days, the course was played to the left on the way out. That is to say, clockwise. Thus, the first hole was near the present location of the 17th green. Actually, the green was situated just over the Swilcan Bridge. Naturally, the hole was tagged with the monicker "The Bridge Hole."

From this first original hole, a player next played to the vicinity of the present 16th green as his second. From there he traversed the course in much the same way that automobile drivers in Great Britain do. They mind the left. And in early days, they played The Old Course backward from the way the course is presently played. You might say those older golfers knew the Old Course backward and forward.

The famous St. Andrews publisher, Robert Chambers, whose house is commemorated by a plaque on The Scores, described the original first hole in the following verse:

The First or Bridge Hole
R.C.

Sacred to hope and promise is the spot –
To Philp's and to the Union Parlour near,
To every Golfer, every caddie dear –
Where we strike off - oh, ne'er to be forgot,
Although in lands most distant we sojourn.
But not without its perils is the place;
Mark the opposing caddie's sly grimace,
Whispering: "He's on the road!" "He's in the burn!"
So is it often in the grander game
Of life, when, eager, hoping for the palm,
Breathing of honour, joy, and love and fame,
Conscious of nothing like a doubt or qualm,
We start, and cry: "Salute us, muse of fire!"
And the first footstep lands us in the mire.

In the days of long-nose, scared-head clubs and feathery golf balls, the left-hand course was an exacting examination of skill. This was owing to the extremely narrow fairways that characterized the earliest course. J.G. McPherson, biographer of Allan Robertson, recalled first-hand these early course conditions: *The links at St. Andrews were then much rougher than I have found them on subsequent visits. There was but one course and the same nine holes served for the outward as for the inward round. Each hole was marked by a small iron pin with a bit of red flag attached. The greens were 'in the rough' and the bunkers were in their natural state. If a player went off the narrow course of good ground he was at once landed in very rough 'country,' and the course at the ninth hole was all heathery and difficult across its whole breadth.* Not only were the same fairways used for holes going out but also for coming to the home hole as well. Golfers got their money's worth of play in those days. That's because they played the same 11 holes out and 11 holes in for a total of 22 holes per round. Someone became economy-minded in 1764 when the first four holes were combined into two holes. That produced an 18-hole course with nine holes out and nine in.

About 1832, a highland chief was struck with the singular notion that double greens should be created to provide much needed elbow room for the numerous golfers. The idea is credited to Aeneas Ronaldson MacDonnell of Glengarry and Clan Ranald. Some even feared the gutty would reduce the Old Course to an elementary exercise of pitch and putt. But as we shall see, there was a little bark left in the old dog yet.

The price of progress was purchased at a cost of not only eight double greens but also a dramatic widening of the course by cutting back and burning off the gnarly whin bushes. Expansion of the once narrow links was described by James Balfour in *Reminiscences of Golf on St. Andrews Links:*

Let us now consider the changes that have taken place on each of the holes individually, and we shall do so by following the medal round, taking the course out by the right.

1. The first hole used always to be on the green beside the road. Its hazards were the road across the Links, the burn, the bunker on one side of the putting-green, as well as the turnpike road on the other—making thus a limited green with a narrow approach to it flanked by severe hazards.

The first hole on the medal round now is quite different. It is placed just beyond the burn, on a flat, smooth, broad green to the right of the course. The only hazards on the hole are the road across the Links and the burn. There are none whatever close to the hole.

2. The tee for the second hole used to be, of course, near the road. There was then no separate teeing-grounds, but the rule was to tee within eight club-lengths of the hole. The ground between the wall and the bunkers towards the corner of the dyke, which is now often preferred as the shortest approach to the hole, was covered with thick whins and was then quite unplayable. Consequently players were obliged to cross the course, and approach the hole by the right of the bunkers. The whins on the right made the course narrow in that direction, and the low ground to the right of the putting-green could not be played on on account of whins and rough grass, so that the hole was much more difficult both in playing and approaching than now. The putting-green, too, which was formerly on a slope, has been made quite level.

At present the tee of this hole is on the right of the Links, while the whins having been driven back, and the low ground to the right near the hole made quite playable, the hole can be played without any bunkers intervening, or any hazards of any kind. Of course if the player goes off the line he has to encounter some hazards. The putting-green, as has been said, is now on a flat and not a slope.

3. There used to be a thick bank of whins all along the left of the course by the side of the present railway, and the whins and rough grass on the right made it necessary to play straight in the centre, where was the Principal's Nose, with its little satellite of "Tam's Coo" (now filled up). The smaller bunker too short of these, presented together with them dangerous traps. There was very little room indeed to pass them on either side. The hole was always in the centre of the green, so that the bunker which crosses the Links beside it had to be played over, else a considerable distance was lost by going to the right or left of it.

101

Major Boothby playing to the Bridge Hole on the left-hand course.
Old Tom Morris is far left and Allan Robertson is on the bridge
in the dark suit.

The tee is now on the right side of the green, and the ball from it is easily played to the right of the Principal's Nose, while the hole being to the right of the putting-green, it is readily approached without crossing the bunker.

4. Formerly the whins encroached so much on either side that it was necessary that the tee stroke should be played on or over the table in front of the tee, and then a very narrow course was left up to the hole, which was on a narrower putting-green than now, and it was usually placed nearer the bunkers.

The whins having been now driven back, the ball can be played to the right of the table. The course is clear for the second stroke, and the hole is placed to the right, far from the bunkers.

5. This hole is more altered than any other on the Links, and sadly destroyed. The tee stroke used always to be played to the right of the big bunker with the uncouth name, unless when now and then some huge driver "swiped over h—— at one immortal go." The second stroke was always to the left on to the Elysian Fields, where the grass was then short and smooth like a putting-green. The third had to navigate the intricate "Beardies," and the fourth was across a wide, staring, horrid bunker, beyond which was a beautiful putting-green. Altogether,

this used to be the finest golfing hole, certainly on the Links, and probably in the world. There were beautiful lies when the play was correct, very difficult hazards, and a perfect putting-green.

Now the play is quite different. The Elysian Fields are avoided, and the hole is played on a lower level, where high whins formerly grew, which made play there impossible. There is hardly any hazard; there are no bunkers of any consideration, and the approach to the green is a blind stroke without any bunker between. The hole is altogether much tamer, and less interesting, as well as easier. The young laird of the Links would do the game of golf an unspeakable benefit if he would plough up the low course, or honeycomb it with bunkers, so as to compel players to return to the old line on the Elysian Fields.

6. The sixth hole is also much altered. It used to be one of the most dangerous on the Links, but two or three large and important bunkers have been filled up to make a double course. This reduces the number of hazards materially, and the whins have so much disappeared that it is safe to go round the bunkers, playing well to the right, instead of being compelled to play over them. The putting-green, too, is greatly changed. Formerly it had no turf, but was merely earth, heather, and shells, from which it got its name of the heather hole, or the "hole o'shell," but is has now been turfed, and, like the other greens, is carefully kept.

7. The course here was a narrow one, so that the first stroke was necessarily played over—very often, unfortunately, into—the bunker that crosses the green; but there was not much room to go on either side of it. The putting-green at the high hole, which was always placed near the Eden, was then surrounded with thick, bent grass, leaving a very limited space near the hole. Besides, the ground was sandy and soft. The deterioration of this putting-green has been averted by the growth of rank sea-grass on the banks of the Eden, which prevents the sand from being blown on to the Links. These bents were a serious hazard.

8. The short hole is not much changed, except that the putting-green is wider than it used to be.

9. On the last hole going out used to be principally heather, but a large portion of that heather was some years ago taken up and relaid with turf. The putting-green is now also much broader than formerly.

The only remaining single greens were the first, ninth, 17th, and 18th. The 17th green was relocated from its original position as the Bridge Hole. It was moved due north and west toward the road in its present location. In 1870, the modern first green—The Burn Hole—was established just over the Swilcan Burn.

The Left-Hand Course comprised of 18 holes continued to be played from about 1864 until 1914 with a slight variation. The Links Committee thought it would be a good idea to preserve the turf and not wear it out by alternating play weekly from the left-hand (clockwise) course to the right-hand (counterclockwise) course.

Therefore, on one week the players would keep to the left and the following week the players would stay to the right. It is interesting to note that more bunkers can be readily seen by players going out on the left-hand course. However, more bunkers on the right-hand course tend to be hidden from the players' view.

Five major championships were played on the left-hand course: The Opens of 1873, 1876, 1879, and 1881. By 1886, it was decided that the Amateur Championship would be contested on the right-hand course. But someone forgot to tell the starter. Because he noticed that the course had been prepared by the greenskeeper for the customary week scheduled for the left-hand course. So play was begun on the left before the authorities could figure out what was happening. The Championship was finished out as it was started. In 1914, the alternating system was discontinued. The left-hand course has been sparingly used since World War II, most recently January 1989.

Thus, the first or Bridge Hole became the penultimate hole on the Old Course. As such, it has provided much drama in championships as well as casual matches.

In recent years the "powers that be" have continued to deal with the problems of increased play on the Old Course, especially after the Railroad Links Line made St. Andrews more easily accessible. But, instead of widening the course even more, or doubling the greens, they decided on a strategy which would preserve the Old Course integrity. They built more golf courses. But none of these new golf holes has ever duplicated the challenges presented by the Road Hole. It is truly *sui generis.*

THE RIDDLE OF THE ROAD

Dr. W.F.G. Deighton, Scottish Internationalist, in trouble at the 17th.

Some riddles are impossible to solve. Try this one: "Which came first, the owl or the egg?" Others seem to be equally hopeless: "Which came first, the Road or the Road Hole?" At an age when the high tides covered this land, the answer is apparent. Unlike the folks who constructed the Old Course Hotel for reasons known only to them to this day, it makes no sense whatsoever to have a road under water. That sentiment changed when the tide receded and golfers began to whack their feather balls up to the hole in the ground that constituted the Bridge Hole.

For many centuries, St. Andrews enjoyed a lengthy reputation for the skill of its "fisher folk." Since the days when the Scots, Anglos, Picts, Culdees, and Saxons may have trod the land, fisher folk practiced their skills in and around St. Andrews. Some estimate that the fishing industry dates back nearly one thousand years. Fishing was a predominant industry until the early nineteenth century. Mussels were cultivated and harvested in the Eden Estuary for centuries until the depressed 1940s economy caused its profitability to suffer. The fisher folk even had their own community known as "Ladyhead." The task fell to Provost Playfair to "reclaim" the fisher folk and

17th. ROAD HOLE
467 yds.

Road
Progressing
Scholars'
Cheapes
Sheds

BOGEY 5   SCORE 8

**CAN YOU BEAT BOGEY
AT ST. ANDREWS?**
SERIES OF 55   CARD NO. 51

MR. RABBIT'S ROUND— 17TH HOLE.

Mr. Rabbit relapsed again here. He hit the drive of his life right over the sheds and that unsettled him. He hooked his second into the Scholar's bunker, smote hard and went right over the green into the road and close to the wall. Here he tried to play a racket shot off the wall. Three. The ball nearly hit him in the stomach and bounded into the Road bunker. Four. Stayed there—five. Nearly into the Road again—six. Two putts. **8.**

Bernard Darwin

For Particulars of a Competition in connection with this card, see the inset enclosed with this packing.
W. A. & A. C. CHURCHMAN, IPSWICH.
Issued by The Imperial Tobacco Company (of Great Britain and Ireland), Limited.

Col. Bogey's cigarette card for the Road Hole.

rescue them from their state of "filth, misery and degradation." He saw to it that "the wretched abodes of filth had been cleaned out, the men led to cherish temperance, and the women to seek after domestic comfort and cleanliness."

Author James K. Robertson reports in his book *St. Andrews - Home of Golf* that the Old Course has been in existence for the playing of golf since at least the 12th century—almost 800 years.

The fisher folk had to have some way to get their catch to market. And it must have been convenient and made sense to them if they could just nip across the land used by the golfers to do it. The question is, where did they do that. During those earliest times, the fisher folk may have forded the Swilcan Burn at whatever point was safest. It wasn't deep water. They then reached perhaps the earliest road leading to the Town of Cupar. The people in Cupar liked to eat the fish and the fisher folk liked to oblige them. This road was so popular and its upkeep important enough that it was made into a toll road about 1800, according to Lord Jo Grimond

Max Marston contemplating his recovery from the Road.

of Firth in his book, *The St. Andrews of Jo Grimond*:

> *Looking down the Swilcan Burn from this point where Gibson Place meets the Links you will see an extremely agreeable little humped bridge made of sandstone. It was not, as I was brought up to believe, built by the Romans but it has been there for a long time, first appearing in seventeenth-century prints.*
>
> *According to the First Statistical account, during the eighteenth century there were only three bridges in the parish of St. Andrews which extended about 10 miles by 4 miles. Two of these were over the Kinness or Ladebraes burn. The third, presumably the one we are looking at, was on the road to Dundee. However, it must only have been used by pack-horses and all trace of a road has disappeared. Presumably the Swilcan, which is rather a miserable, though historic, burn was normally crossed by a ford. Mr. Burnet, the historian of the Royal and Ancient, thinks that the bridge was probably used principally by fish merchants taking fish from St. Andrews harbour to Cupar. The original road seems to have run further south so that it is doubtful whether 'the golfers' bridge' was*

Fred Couples in the Road.

used by pedestrians or pack-horses. The roadway, which gives its name to the seventeenth hole (the Road Hole), later became a turnpike or toll road in about 1800. The bridge may therefore have always been intended for the use of golfers.

It was then known as the Turnpike Road. The Road is also labeled "Turnpike from Cupar" on the first survey of the Old Course prepared in 1836 by Mr. Chalmers from Perth, reproduced in J.B. Salmond's book *The Story of the R&A* at page 5. In 1823 the Town Council, with the approval of the newly reconstituted Links

Committee, built a lifeboat house between the Swilcan Burn and a feu on the south edge of the first fairway on the Turnpike Road.

There were several informal roads or lanes which sprang from the Turnpike Road and coursed to the area of the Eden River Estuary. They were alternate routes for fisher folk to connect to the Turnpike Road to Cupar. One of these was called the "Mussel Road." It cut across just west of the golf course land and connected to the estuary so that the mussels could be hauled out, perhaps by pack animals.

Today there is a vestige of the old Mussel Road opposite the 17th tee and running roughly in front of the Old Course Hotel. There is a "fingerpoint" sign on the first tee of the Eden course which points in the direction of the old Mussel Road. The "fingerpoint" sign reads "Beware of golf balls." The old Mussel Road was slightly diverted during the improvements to the Eden course. The use of this informal Mussel Road by the fisher folk did not apparently ingratiate them to Provost Playfair, who vigorously contended they were damaging the surrounding grounds. So he strongly discouraged its use. Although it is apparently the consensus of ancient survey maps that the road immediately behind the Road Hole green is indeed the Turnpike Road to Cupar, nonetheless it has been confused with the Mussel Road located some distance further west from the Road Hole green. Indeed, the local rule defining the road as a "hazard" as late as 1951 referred to it as the Mussel Road, to wit:

1. The Swilcan Burn.—The portion of the Swilcan Burn running parallel to the fairway of the first hole and defined by white posts is a lateral water hazard. Rule 36(3) applies.

2. The 17th Hole (Old Course):

> *(a) Along the 17th fairway the grass between the Mussel Road and the wall is part of the hazard.*
>
> *(b) At the 17th green the bank leading down to the gravel footpath is not part of the hazard, but all the rest of the ground between the bank and the wall is part of the hazard.*

It is unfortunate that confusion may have sprung from the above misdescription. Because almost one hundred years earlier in 1852, Provost Playfair caused the Mussel Road to be blocked off due to the building of the Links Railway Station adjacent to the 17th fairway. The Mussel Road no longer junctioned to the Turnpike Road in the vicinity of the Road Hole green. A pedestrian bridge was then built over the railway and connecting pedestrians to the Turnpike Road from the golf course. Historian James Balfour in his *Reminiscences of Golf on St. Andrews Links* published in 1887 confirmed that the Turnpike Road is the road behind the Road Hole green:

The first hole used always to be on the green side of the road. Its hazards were the road across the links, the burn, the bunker on one side of the putting

green, as well as the Turnpike road on the other—making this a limited green with a narrow approach to it flanked by severe hazards.

Balfour's reference to the "road across the links" is to Granny Clarks Wynd. It used to be called "Sandy Track" a century ago, according to author Douglas Young in his work *St. Andrews Town & Gown, Royal and Ancient* (p. 225). It constituted a considerable hazard in the early centuries, especially when wagons and horses slogged across it causing sizeable depressions, ruts, and sludge. Golf balls don't marry well with golf clubs in such circumstances. It was only golfers' ingenuity that solved the problem of that marriage. Voilà! Thus was born the rut or track iron.

There was another path across the links and over the Swilcan Burn bridge. Some historians including Bobby Burnet surmise that the golfer's bridge was also used by the fisher folk hauling their catch from St. Andrews harbour to Cupar. Others, principally Lord Jo Grimond, explain the contrary view that "the golfer's bridge" was so "aptly named that it is doubtful pedestrians or pack-horses debouched it with their base labors and activities." Being intended for the use of golfers, he is confident that it has always probably and principally been used by golfers.

Lord Grimond seems to have made a good observation on this point. There are myriad photographs and paintings of golfers standing on the Swilcan Burn bridge in existence even today. These images date back to the eighteenth century. But when is the last time you ever saw a painting or photograph of two fisher folk standing on the Swilcan Burn bridge, proudly stretching a stringer of fish between them? Clearly, golfers are a "tribe aparte" from mere fisher folk. But that is a different riddle from the Riddle of the Road.

For many years, the Turnpike Road was comprised of loose cinders and gravel. The footpath on the edge of the road was also a loose irregular surface. Journalist Malcolm Campbell has observed in recent times, however, that the character of the road's maintenance has been altered:

Sadly in 1998, the powers-that-be saw fit to entirely cover over the old road with tar macadam and by so doing remove the rough and stony ground at the bottom of the bank behind the green which was so much part of the character of the hole. It was an act of vandalism which those with any understanding of the place could scarcely believe. However, it remains as ever a threat to be avoided at all costs.

We should add "Amen" to this.

Billy Casper playing from the Road Bunker.

THE ROAD BUNKER

When the Road Hole green was relocated to its present position around 1764, "a greedy little bunker that eats its way into the very vitals of the green" became an instant threat to the sanity of all golfers. Prior to that time, the present Road Bunker did not exert a particularly menacing influence upon the original Bridge Hole Green located just over the Swilcan Burn Bridge. In order to get in trouble playing the left-hand course to the original Bridge Hole, a player had to strongly overshoot the green to be captured by the Bunker.

The advent of the gutta-percha ball caused a series of events to unfold. First, the gutta-percha ball made the game much more popular because it flew further. More people began to play, and the powers that be took two important steps to accommodate the increased popularity. Instead of creating new holes, the existing greens were enlarged to make double greens with two holes on each. The ancient golf course was expanded to accommodate more frequent play with a friskier golf ball, and that created a second problem that needed to be solved. Surely the course would be worn out by the influx of many more players. After all, until 1913 local inhabitants and visitors alike played for free. Townspeople and "ratepayers" continued to play free until 1946. To solve the problem, it was decided that the right-hand course and the left-hand courses would be alternated each week, except during the peak golfing season.

Thus, it was announced in 1856 that:

In consequence of the golfing course being much out of order by the greatly increased number of golfers and smashing with clicks, the Royal and Ancient deemed it necessary to vote a sum of 25 pounds to have the turf and bunkers repaired. Although just about half the sum is yet laid out the course wears a better look...Along with this is another improvement, viz., two holes in each putting green, with the exception of the first and end hole, white flags going out and red ones coming in. The bent and whins have been cleared to widen the course when necessary.

In the nineteenth century, the Old Course continued to alternate between the left-hand and right-hand courses, while changing the routing every two weeks. The Open was played on the left-hand course on four occasions in 1873, 1876, 1879 and 1881. One of the chief proponents of using the alternating routing system was the

Links Committee which directed Old Tom Morris, Keeper of the Green, to use his best efforts to prevent constant wear and tear on the greens and fairways. It was also Old Tom Morris who enforced the decree that golf should not be played on Sundays, stating, "Weel, sir, the links want a rest on the Sabbath, even if you don't."

In 1924, distinguished golf architect Alister MacKenzie was commissioned to prepare a survey map of the Old Course. It took him a year to complete the task. After that, he knew the course as well as anyone. In 1920, MacKenzie had published a book on golf architecture. And he was not well known for rationing his speech when it came to expressing opinions about how golf courses should be designed

Jack Nicklaus playing from the Road Bunker.

and maintained. MacKenzie believed that trees had no purpose on the golf course. And he said that long grass was of little interest as a hazard. Instead, he urged that undulating ground consisting of hillocks and hollows should be employed to the maximum to provide interest in the routing of golf holes.

On the subject of bunkers, MacKenzie's views were not wishy-washy. In his lost manuscript, *The Spirit of St. Andrews* written in 1934, MacKenzie wrote:

Ordinary bunkers, as a rule, are made in quite the wrong way. The face is usually too upright and the ball gets into an unplayable position under the face. The bottom of the bank of a bunker should have a considerable slope so that a ball always rolls toward the middle. The top of a bunker may, as it usually does in nature, be made to overhang a little so that a topped ball may be prevented from running through it.

*   *   *

As a rule, hazards are placed too far away from the green they are intended to guard. They should be placed immediately on the edge of the green and then, particularly if they are in the form of smooth hillocks and hollows, the player who is wide of them has an extremely difficult pitch and is frequently worse off than the man who is among them.

As a golf course architect with considerable knowledge of the Old Course, MacKenzie held up to the world the example of St. Andrews' Road Bunker as one which accomplishes every task which might be assigned to it:

A bunker eating into a green is by far the most equitable way of giving a golfer full advantage for accurate play. It not only penalizes the man who is in it but also everyone who is wide of it. For example, a player who is in the "Road bunker" at the seventeenth at St. Andrews may, with a good explosion shot, get out and lie dead, but few can pitch over it so accurately that they can do so. A bunker similarly placed to the Road bunker may be made to accentuate this distinction. It may be constructed with so much slope that on occasions it may be possible to putt out of it.

The favorite adjective used by some to describe this sand pit is "beastly." It is at once a term of endearment and the vilest oath. If the Road bunker does one thing, it is to summon every emotion known to mankind and to burn those emotions on the player's mind and heart for generations to follow.

Bob Jones from the 17th tee.

The black sheds are just over Don Moe's shoulder.

THE RAILWAY

Prior to 1852, anyone who traveled to the medieval city of St. Andrews couldn't say they got there by way of the railroad line. There wasn't any then. It was likely a great day in 1829 when the first stagecoach began running to and from St. Andrews. The stage went once a week to Cupar and twice a week to Dundee. As the popularity of the University grew and as the city's commerce increased, fueled in no small part by the golf course, more people clamored to visit St. Andrews.

By the time Rev. Charles Roger published his history of the city in 1849, the Edinburgh and Northern Railway had extended its tracks and service from the Forth port of Burntisland via nearby Leuchars Station, to Ferryport-on-Craig on the Tay. Horse-drawn coaches and omnibuses were also providing daily runs to St. Andrews from Edinburgh via Leuchars Junction.

Geologist Richard Batchelor, who has studied the history of the railway as a hobby, tells us that the St. Andrews Railway Company conducted its preliminary organizational meeting on January 29, 1850. The purpose, of course, was to extend the railway line from Leuchars to St. Andrews. This was accomplished by an Act of Parliament passed on July 3, 1851 entitled "The St. Andrews Railway." Immediately after its passage, work began extending the tracks to St. Andrews. The opening of the St. Andrews Railway from Leuchars Junction to St. Andrews Links Station, a distance of 4.5 miles, was celebrated on July 1, 1852. The traffic created by the opening of Links Station was considerable. For instance, on July 7, 1852, there were four daily passenger trains to and from Edinburgh connecting through the Leuchars Junction. There were four trains traveling daily from St. Andrews to Dundee and Perth. Further, St. Andrews received three trains daily from Dundee and Perth. There were a total of 18 passenger train movements each day. The revenues generated by the new St. Andrews Railway Company line was substantial. During the month of January 1860, the railway generated almost 2,000 pounds (passenger: 1,043 pounds; goods and minerals: 858 pounds; parcels and livestock: 67 pounds; rents: 17 pounds). The Links Station was built on the present site of the Old Course Hotel on the west side of the 17th fairway. The original Stationmaster's house remains today as the Jigger Inn. One anonymous member of the R&A memorialized the influx of visitors to the links in his 1854 verse "St. Andrews To The Play":

St. Andrews' banner nobly flew;
Matches an' bets were not a few;
Excursion trains poured in amain
Gentle 'an semple swelled the train.
Lean wabsters frae Dunfermline,
Folk frae Fife's sea-side toons that shine
Like chance-dropt pearls beside the brine;
While Cupar lads were no abint
To see the Medal won and tint.

Originally the Links Station operated to carry both passengers, goods and freight. One important imported resource was coal. Next to the Links Station stood a barn-like structure known as the coal sheds or black sheds. There was a brisk business conducted by coal carts traveling to and from the coal sheds. These black sheds were situated at an angle as one looked at them from the 17th tee. Veteran golf journalist Peter Dobereiner recalled the first occasion he saw them while playing the Old Course:

At last on the 17th tee, we had a secular landmark for the target line. Hit your drive directly over the letter "D", he commanded, indicating the name "Anderson" painted on the roof of the old railway sheds. I went one better and my ball hit the letter "D" fairly and squarely, rebounding into oblivion. I remember, with a pang of shame, that I subsequently described the Old Course as a "sad old bitch of a golf course" in the public prints.

In the days of hickory-shafted drivers and gutta-percha balls, it was a formidable challenge to risk the long carry over the corner of the black sheds and into the fairway beyond. Even when the hole played as a par 5, the safe line was to the left on the drive. Then the player could try to negotiate his next approach to the front-right of the green.

In 1887, the railway was extended into the city center chiefly for the transport of passengers and formed a new rail link with the Fife Coast line. The train was the predominant mode of transportation to the city up to World War II. Cabs, buses, bicycles, and horses then were used to get around once inside the city.

When the new city center passenger station was established in 1887 on the Anstruther extension, the old original terminal was converted to a freight depot for goods commerce only. (Today the site of the new station of 1887 is a car park adjacent to the bus station.) Business became even more brisk when the Forth Railway Bridge

opened in 1890. This continued up to the Second World War when the automobile was popularized and train traffic diminished. Just before the war, steel shafts and rubber-core golf balls became the rage and would have helped the golfers on the Road Hole immeasurably except for another change to the Road Hole landscape. Large storage sheds were constructed adjacent to the railway goods yard. These storage sheds were in place when Bobby Jones won the first leg of his immortal Grand Slam in 1930. In his memoirs, Jones fondly recalled launching his drives from the 17th tee over these sheds. In his autobiography, *Golf is My Game*, Jones wrote:

As will be seen from the drawing, the drive must be over a low-lying shed. In my day, the side of the shed nearer the tee bore the name "D. Anderson" in letters more than a foot high. The proper line on my occasions was over the "little d" in Anderson. Playing in the Walker Cup foursomes in 1926, Andrew Jamieson plunked his tee shot solidly into the side of the shed, out of bounds, so that his partner, Cyril Tolley, had to return some hundred yards from the corner of the fence, which he did in a majestic grandeur, exuding indignation from every pore. This started a comical sequence which ended when my partner, Watts Gunn, and I won the hole in seven.

In golf there is a fairly general aversion to blind shots. I don't especially mind blind tee shots such as this one, because the "little d" in Anderson and a familiarity with the skyline of the town provide sufficient guideposts. Blind shots to the green, when it is not possible to know the exact location of the flag, are entirely different.

The tee in those days, was in the very corner of the fence alongside the railroad. Now, in order to provide passageway for spectators in connection with the modern "crowd-control," the tee has been moved nearer the second green. The hole may be as good, but it simply is not the same to me.

In 1930, a sign on the sheds announced "D&W Auchterlonie Timber Drying Sheds." The Andersons and later Auchterlonies used the sheds for the drying of hickory shafts used in making golf clubs. The firm of D&W Auchterlonie was established by Willie Auchterlonie, the 1893 Open Champion. His brother David also joined the firm. By 1901, the firm of "D&W Auchterlonie" was recognized as "one of the best firms in the golf club making trade." The firm was located at Albany Place in St. Andrews. Willie was appointed honorary professional to the Royal & Ancient Golf Club in 1935 until his death in 1963. Even after D. Anderson & Sons reconfigured partners in 1926, the sheds continued to be used for the purpose of drying hickory shafts. Behind the black sheds in 1930 was a practice field. And on that side of the sheds facing the

Jack Nicklaus playing from the 17th tee.

practice field was painted "D&W Auchterlonie Timber Drying Sheds" in white letters. Photographs of Bobby Jones in 1930 practicing in this field confirm this fact. But as late as 1930, the name "D. Anderson & Sons" was still visible on the black sheds from the Road Hole tee.

Author Douglas Young further described what subsequently happened to the letters on the sheds:

Til 1967, there were black sheds on the right of the tee which the bold drivers used to carrying, aiming to soar over the second letter "d" of the name "D. Anderson," which was painted there until 1940, when the prudent citizens obliterated it, for fear that Adolf Hitler might parachute in and realize he was at the seventeenth hole.

It should be explained that "D. Anderson" referred to David Anderson, Jr. (1847-1912) who was the son of "Old Daw" Anderson, a legendary ball maker, green keeper, and caddie. David Jr. opened his own club-making enterprise called "D. Anderson & Sons," operated under that name from 1895 until 1926. David had five sons in the business, too. One son named David was runner-up in the 1888 Open to Jack Burns.

More than one prominent professional golfer remembers riding the St. Andrews Railway Line from Leuchars Junction. Sam Snead still recalls his first ride on the train from Edinburgh to Leuchars to St. Andrews in 1946 when he won the Open Championship in his maiden attempt. He was sitting across from a proper gentleman wearing a hat. Snead recalls looking out of the window and seeing what he perceived to be a run-down golf course:

The grass was all scroggly and the greens looked like they weren't maintained, and the bunkers looked like they had never been raked. And I asked the gentleman sitting across from me, "What old abandoned golf course is that?" And the gentleman took off his hat and stood up with a horrified look on his face and said "I'll have you know that's the Royal and Ancient Golf Club of St. Andrews!"

In the 1960s, the British Transport Authority proposed to raze the black sheds and build an extravagant "state of the art" modern hotel on the property. This was not just a run-of-the-mill hotel. A passenger would be afforded the luxury of stepping off the train where a lift would take him up to the registration desk to check into the hotel. A porter would collect his valise and golf clubs and carry them up to the guest's waiting room. The passenger would not even have to walk outside into the elements. But this grand scheme never happened. The controversy over the granting of permission has yet to abate three decades later. Historian Keith Mackie noted in his history of *Golf at St. Andrews: In the space of less than two years St. Andrews had gained an ugly hotel and lost its link to the national rail network*. Others called the hotel an act of *vandalism, barbarism and a landscape wrecker*. It has also been called "ugly, graceless and out of scale." The fact is, when permission was finally granted, British Railways decided to close the railway from Leuchars Junction to St. Andrews due to lack of profit. But the last train to St. Andrews ran on January 4th 1969 and it was full! It is questionable whether permission to build the "chest of drawers" looking building on such a historic site would have passed muster under the new Land Use Planning Act's stringent requirements enacted some years later in 1973.

Not only did the high-rise hotel radically encroach the air space on the Road Hole, but insult was added to injury when the black sheds were pulled down. It seems that, although so many players had suffered at the challenge of negotiating the black sheds from the tee, they were outraged when the quirky challenge was eliminated. The hotel developers tried to assuage the bitter criticism by building a metal mesh skeleton in the shape of the former black sheds on the same site where the sheds used to stand. The trellis-type fence was supposed to provide the player on the 17th tee a *virtual perspective* intended to mirror the profile and roof outline and thus impose the same challenge presented by the original black sheds. While perhaps born of sincere intentions, the artificial structure was not favorably received. So in 1978, the developers built a realistic replica of the black sheds using materials which better simulate the original building. But instead of replacing the

The Railway Line adjacent to the 17th tee and 16th green.

"D. Anderson & Sons" sign on the wall of the building, the developers put the hotel's name "St. Andrews Old Course & Hotel."

After the hotel opened in 1968, it was twice sold to newly constituted consortiums. In 1990, the hotel exterior was modified from the aesthetically displeasing "chest of drawers" design.

There's one person who might have shouted "good riddance" when the charming old railroad went away. He is James Braid, who was the first man to win five Open Championships. In the 1905 Open Championship, James twice drove his ball onto the railroad tracks, which was not deemed to be out-of-bounds, but rather, part of the course. And the rule was you play the ball as it lies. At the 15th, James sliced his ball onto the tracks. He did well to hit the ball off the tracks, but it then hit a spectator and rebounded into a gorse bush. That cost him a six.

On the next hole, Braid hit a cracker from the tee which carried an awesome distance over the cruel Principal's Nose bunker. After a few bounces, however, it ended in Deacon Sime's tiny crevice. His lie looked good enough. So James tried a stroke that was admittedly "too venturesome" toward the green. His ball ended up

on the railroad tracks once again for the second consecutive hole. "I found it lying in a horrible place," Braid said, "being tucked up against one of the iron chairs in which the rails rest, it was on the left-hand side of the right-hand rail, playing towards the hole, and the only crumb of comfort was that it was not on the other side of either of the rails. I took my niblick and tried to hook it out, but did not succeed, the ball moving only a few yards, and being in much the same position against the rail. With my fourth, however, I got it back on the course, but in a very difficult position." Braid got down in 6 and got past the Road Hole, winning by five strokes from Rowland Jones and J.H. Taylor.

Perhaps Braid would be one of a few who would agree that it was no great loss to see the railroad become extinct. On the other hand, Andra Kirkaldy may have decried the closing of the railroad for a special reason. When Andra was caddying for a hapless player, his man's ball became hopelessly bunkered. The player looked forlorn as he turned to Kirkaldy and inquired, "What should I do now?" Kirkaldy paused not a moment to reply, "If I were you, I'd take the 9:40 train out of St. Andrews."

The Stationmaster's House, now serving as The Jigger.

THE STATIONMASTER'S HOUSE AND GARDEN

The Railway Stationmaster's House and Garden were built by 1854 when the Links Station was established adjacent to the western part of the 17th fairway. It is a handsome two-story white painted house which now serves as the "Jigger Inn."

As a boy, Lord Grimond of Firth recalled the men who operated the railway in St. Andrews:

The rail officials were well known and respected local figures: the station master, Lees; the guard, Haddow; and Docherty, the foreman porter. Haddow was typical of the St. Andrews functionaries. Immaculate in uniform and peaked cap he resembled a rather stout Sir Walter Scott. Docherty was more of Stevenson's build and colouring, and wore his cap on the back of his head. Both were men of standing and authority. I am glad that the spirit of the old railway men, helpful and humorous, still persists. Traveling recently in Fife in one of those trains laughably called Sprinters, I asked the ticket collector if it stopped at the Haymarket station in Edinburgh. 'Oh yes', he replied, 'it stops at every lamp-post.' When a boy I was reprimanded by Haddow for crossing the line to collect a starling's egg from a nest in the wall of the cutting. That evening after dark, Haddow called at our house and taking off his cap produced four eggs out of its crown. Quite a few people commuted to and from Dundee, either to University College, Dundee, then a part of St. Andrews University, or to work in Dundee offices and mills. City Park, the house which looks down on the railway from the east, is another of Rae's designs.

Another local man who worked for most of his life on the local railways was Willie Paul. For a number of years, he worked as the signalman at the Links Box. He is seen in one surviving photograph "exchanging tablets" to allow the 2:20 p.m. Dundee train into St. Andrews.

Playing from The Swilcan Burn to the first green.

WEE BONNIE BURN
VS.
DOMMED SEWER

The Swilcan Burn is a distinguishing feature of the present-day 1st and 18th holes. Since Halket's Bunker was covered over in the decade after 1836, the Swilcan Burn constituted the principal hazard at the first hole of the left-hand course. In his history on St. Andrews, author Douglas Young describes the origins of the Burn:

A century ago, the Swilcan wandered whither it willed, through sandy banks that were frequently altered by occasional spates. Today it is canalized between vertical banks, at widths varying from about five feet to about twelve. The humpback stone bridge over the Burn on the 18th fairway is some centuries old.

Historian J.B. Salmond in his work on *The Story of the R.&A.* helps to complete the lineage of the Burn:

Mr. W.T. Linskill, writing in Chambers's Journal (dated 1/8/1906), states that in the early 'seventies when he used to play with Young Tom Morris between the Royal and Ancient Golf Club and the burn at the first hole, many acres of land have been reclaimed from the German Ocean. Where I can remember the seashore once existed, there are now excellent lies for the players' balls. There are, I believe, three sea-walls buried under the golf green, and the old bathing-place was once under the present window of the north room of the Club. The historic Swilcan Burn formerly swept almost into the centre of the Links before it turned into the sea, and one often drove into this bed from the first tee. It was then a sandy natural hazard, but now it is a concrete-walled channel.

A lifeboat station was situated adjacent to the Burn. That's the same lifeboat that golfer Maitland Dougall used to help rescue some sad fellows whose boat foundered in the bay in 1860. Dougall was playing in the Autumn Medal when the rescue alarm was sounded. He put down his clubs and took a laboring oar for the apparently successful five-hour interruption from his game. One would think that any right-minded fellow might call it a day after the lifeboat returned and subsequently repair to the 19th hole for a wee nip and bowl of porridge. But Dougall had unfinished business to attend. He resumed his round without skipping a beat and won the Club Gold Medal, returning a score of 112 strokes. All that in a day's work.

Reverend Charles Roger described the Burn in his 1849 *History of St. Andrews*:

127

Bob Jones negotiating the Burn.

The links which extend from the west end of the town to the mouth of the Eden are about two miles in length, and for the purpose of golfing have generally been reckoned to be the best in the kingdom. They are possessed of numerous inequalities and sand-pits, which are said by golfers to add life and interest to their game. At the eastern part, the links are intersected by the Swilcan Burn, a considerable rivulet, in which unpractical golfers occasionally drive their balls.

But not everyone has been enamored with the romantic description provided by historians. In fact, Horace Hutchison called it a distasteful streamlet and a "sorry little burn that traps balls." Then he administered the coup de grace calling it:

A muddy little dribble worming along ignominiously at a crawl between little stone built walls as if it would never get to the sea.

One significant tributary adjacent to the Old Course is the Eden River. On the other hand, the Swilcan Burn originates about three miles west from the Road Hole in the town of Strathkiness. The stream has been less commonly called Swilcan-The-Burn and Jackson's Burn.

In the early nineteenth century the meandering stream had no well-defined banks and was easily forded by golfers. In the winter it was prone to swell. Finally, in the 1900s, initial work was done to shore up its banks. At first railway sleepers were used. Over the years, considerable work has been carried out to permanently establish the banks and prevent erosion.

The Swilcan Burn could be driven from the first tee on the left-hand course when the Bridge Hole was in play. The fairway was severely restricted as well and Halket's bunker was a third significant hazard with which to negotiate.

The Swilcan Burn has not always been full enough with water to prevent a player from attempting to play a stroke from its banks. In the early 1920s, the 1924 British Amateur Champion Cyril Tolley's ball landed on a spit of gravel in the burn. Down into the burn he went with a niblick and played a marvelous stoke onto the green not far from the flagstick. As late as 1989, Christy O'Connor, Jr. successfully played his ball out of the burn, playing the first hole during the Dunhill Cup.

In his memoirs, architect Alister MacKenzie described his philosophy about the value of water hazards:

I was once playing with my brother, who was home on leave from abroad. He was clearly enjoying his game, but at Alwoodley we have one solitary pond into which he topped three balls. On arriving back at the clubhouse he was asked how he liked the course. His only remark about it was, "You've got too many ruddy ponds about." The use of a water hazard is a very debatable question. Being a Scotsman, I am naturally opposed to water in its undiluted state. I am also opposed to a hazard involving the risk of a lost ball.

On the other hand, I am very much in favour of utilizing water where it exists as a natural feature, particularly if there is a clean bottom and there is a chance of recovering one's ball. Players also get such a tremendous thrill driving over the ocean at the spectacular 16th and 17th holes at Cypress Point that this also is well worth the risk of losing a ball or two. I recently crossed over from England with an American who told me that the 16th at Cypress Point had cost him a fortune in golf balls, as he would always play for the long carry to the green across the ocean, but the joy of seeing his ball land on the green and the feeling of something achieved when it did so was worth all the balls he put into

Repairs to the Wee Bonnie Burn

the ocean in his attempts to drive the hazard.

Most folks have little difficulty negotiating the Swilcan Burn since it is not very wide and not very deep. Nevertheless, historian Alister Beaton Adamson records a humorous episode taken from Allan Robertson's golfing album of perhaps the most calamitous crossing of the Swilcan Burn. One of Allan Robertson's feather-ball makers was also a distinguished caddie named Willie Robertson, also known as "Lang Willie." The reason he was called this nickname was owing to his 6´2˝ frame, adorned by a tall top hat called a "lum." It was said that a feather ball was made by stuffing a lum hat full of feathers into a bull-hide cover, but that is another story. Historian James Balfour described Lang Willie as "about 6´2˝, with bent knees and a sloughing gait, a tall hat, swallow-tailed blue coat, and light trousers. His look was rather stupid, but in reality he was wide awake. He used to insist that he drank nothing but sweet milk, greatly to the amusement of Allan, who knew better." The

following account, dated November 1853, was found in Allan Robertson's album entitled "Crossing the Swilcan - A Falling in by the Way:"

On Tuesday afternoon a gentleman who had been engaged in golfing, was about to leave by railway, and devolved the carrying out of luggage, from the Union parlour to the station, upon that venerable member of caddiedom - Long Willie - who, having pressed a wheel barrow into his service, got under weigh.

He was advised to take the route by the high road, but being enamoured of a near cut by crossing the Swilcan burn, Willie made for one of the foot bridges, and had just entered upon it, when lo! shouts of laughter burst from groups of gentlemen, caddies and others about the Parlour — Willie's carriage had got off the rails, and the wheel into the burn, while Willie, saving himself from going the same destination by holding by barrow shafts, had the pleasure of seeing each and all of the traps - a golf club box, gun case, portmanteau, hat-box, and plaid—launch into the water, which was considerably swollen, and sail away towards the ocean.

Assistance being at hand, however, the goods and gear were arrested in transitu seawards, some of them not improved by the hydropathic treatment, though, we believe, the contents of the portmanteau were fortunately scatheless. The rueful countenance Willie assumed, and his intimation that he had got a "gey fricht," increased the merriment that arose among the onlookers at witnessing his exploit, the hero thereof apparently more concerned at his own escape than at any injury the barrow's contents had sustained.

One of Alister MacKenzie's favorite stories about the Swilcan Burn concerned a golfer who asked his caddy what others thought about the wee streamlet. The pawky caddy replied: "Weel, we've got an old Scottish major here who, when he gets ower it says 'Weel ower the bonnie wee burn ma laddie! but when he gets into it he says 'Pick ma ba oot o' that dommed sewer."

Two views of Scholar's Bunker

THE FORGOTTEN BUNKERS: 'CHEAPE'S,' 'SCHOLAR'S' AND 'PROGRESSING'

The Road Hole Bunker is not the only bunker that presents a challenge on the 17th. A tee shot smothered and pulled left may end up in Cheape's bunker which lies about 190 yards straight down the left side. This bunker is named for James Cheape of Strathtyrum, whose family owned the Old Course from 1821 until selling it to the Royal & Ancient Golf Club in 1893. The citizens subsequently applied for a Parliamentary Order forming The Links Trust and providing for local control by the R&A and Links Trust.

On the other hand, a conservative tee shot which does not cut off the corner of the black sheds may end up in the tall grass, the worst of which is called bents, bordering the fairway. Especially when it's wet, a long stroke from here is often misplayed. There is a tendency for the long grass to close the face of the club, and the stroke does not permit the ball to fly out. Even if it does, the ball tends to go to the left. That's just where the Scholar's bunker is. Scholar's rests about 80 yards in front of the green. When the left-hand course was played, the Scholar's bunker was a menace on the second hole going out. An unconfirmed legend states that when a student drove with his hickory-shafted play club and featherie or gutty ball, it was considered a "feather in his cap" to carry Scholar's bunker.

Architect MacKenzie had his doubts about the strategic location of Scholar's bunker:

I often think that the hole would be more interesting without the Scholar's bunker; this prevents a badly hit second getting into the danger zone. If it were not there, one would much more frequently be forced to play the sporting approach to the green with the Road bunker intervening.

Located just in front of Scholar's bunker is "Progressing" bunker. That is what the player does when he misplays his stroke from the bottom of Scholar's bunker. He "progresses" into the next bunker. Once in the Progressing bunker, he can play into the Road Bunker and win the trifecta for bunkers. That's also when the men in white coats come to collect the man at the end of the day. Perhaps that is why historian, Patric Dickinson said the Road Hole is:

Where the last sandcastle of your golfing pride and hope must stand against the waves until you are safely on the eighteenth tee.

133

A freshly revetted Road Bunker awaits the next challenger.

THE DEIL'S SWAIL

The depression in the front-left of the Road Hole green is a Devil's Swail. It acts like a ladle to scoop up timidly stroked balls and pour them helplessly into the sandy bowl known as the Road Bunker. It is in the shape of a concave depression for good reason. Because that is the emotional state bequeathed to anyone who suffers its peril. Consider the psychological effect imparted by this swail. A player who reaches the front of the green is likely in a positive state of mind. He thinks himself lucky not to have suffered the consequences of the Road Bunker and the Road itself. If he has been victimized by previous holes, his spirits are instantly lifted. He has been through Hell, bit off the Principal's Nose, raised a Cockle or two, lost Spectacles, been sized for Coffins, gently extricated from the Lion's Mouth, roughed up in Mrs. Kruger's Kitchen, and even had a few Cheape thrills along the journey.

No wonder his emotional state has reached its zenith upon learning the ball is safely in the bosom of the Road Hole green. It is then that disaster hatches a cruel plan. The player's instinctual response for fear and flight is first disarmed. A false sense of security is substituted.

Then visual deception kicks in. A wide expanse of green 25 feet across makes the player supremely confident his strokes can be made through the Devil's Swail onto the top plateau where the hole awaits. Some fools may even mock the task saying, "piece of cake" or "child's play." He debases and denigrates the feature of the green he has been warned repeatedly to treat with respect and handle with kid gloves. He puffs himself up with pride that he is blessed compared to his companions who apply their agricultural swings extricating their balls from the Bunker and the Road. "Poor Bastards," he softly whispers. "Maybe they should take up tennis." Confidence is at high tide when the stroke is played.

Up to now, Old Ane* has convinced the player that nothing can deter him from achieving the object of his desires. But wait! As the player has settled over his ball and drawn back his putter, the small sarcastic voice of Auld Clubfoot* intones: "I lied, you fool." "What," you reply. "Don't interrupt me now! Can't you see I'm in the middle of my stroke and half a breath away from tasting the sweet nectar of victory?" Auld Nick* is relentless:

(*Scots for Deil or Devil)

135

The Devil's Swail

I told you before you could do it. Nothing could stand in your way. Not height, nor depth, nor hardship, nor persecution, nor rain, nor wind, nor the speed of the green, nor the Leuchars Air Show. But I lied. You are actually unworthy. You can't do it. There's no way you can do it. You don't have the skills. You don't have the intestinal fortitude. You don't deserve it. And, by the way, your ball is in exactly the wrong location on the green to do it. In fact, it can't be done. Even Arnold Palmer couldn't do it from where you are. And you are blinded by your false pride from seeing your peril. You are not even going to keep this ball on the green. It's going somewhere you don't want it to go. And you can't do anything about it. So go ahead and finish your stroke, old chap. Instead of Triumph, you are going to face Disaster. I guarantee it. And I am going to love it when you go down in flames.

In the twinkle of an eye, every ounce of confidence leaks out of his vessel. Whereas before, he was "drinking from his saucer cause his cup was overflowed,

"now he is empty. Panic strikes. But it either strikes too much or not enough. He is helpless. In his innermost being and heart of hearts, he knows that the Deceiver* is right. He is unworthy. He is skill-less. He is hapless. And worst of all, he is alone. Before, Dame Fortune stood beside him. Where did she go? Now it's just the player standing twixt the Deil and the deep green sea.

The player notices something is wrong with his eyes now. He is having a hell of a time seeing the line. It's as though pennies have been placed on his eyelids. Oh, my. Fare for passage across the river Styx!

The player has reached a fork in the road of his fate. He takes it. "I'll fight back," he assures himself with false bravado. "I could coddle the beast and wear him down before I slay him. But I think instead, I'll thrust my sword quickly into the neck of the Dragon and end it without further adieu." He raps the ball harder than intended. Oh for gosh sakes. Too hard. It's in the road. He's dead.

Another player may take the alternative fork of chance. The double-cross. He suspects that the Deceiver* is conjuring him into hitting his ball too strongly. "I'll outwit the buggar," he reasons. "I'll coax it up the Swail and lay the damn thing stone dead. At least I'll get it close enough to still be putting on the next stroke. And then I'll end it." He hits the putt too easy. His ball takes off like the tiny ball going around and around the roulette wheel. When the centrifugal force relents, the ball gradually loses speed and falls like a meteor from the heavens. Oh gimme a break. It's in the Road Bunker. Dead again. Bring the men in the white coats to take him away.

He will need considerable therapy now for his manic-depression. And to reset his emotional compass so that he can once again appreciate one reality of the Road Hole. It is as certain as the stars fixed in the sky, in that plot of ground known as the Deil's Swail, only one power rules. Guess who?

THE ROAD HOLE BIBLIOGRAPHY

Adamson, Alistair Beaton; *Allan Robertson, Golfer: His Life and Times* (Bigwood and Staple Limited Bridgwater, Somerset, 1985)

Akiyama, Masakuni; *Visiting the Home of Golf St. Andrews* (Sun Art of America, Inc., May 1988)

Balfour, James; *Reminiscences of Golf on St. Andrews Links* (Edinburgh 1887)

Behrend, John and Peter N. Lewis; *Challenges & Champions - The Royal & Ancient Golf Club 1754 - 1883* (Henry Ling Ltd., Dorchester, 1998)

Behrend, John; *The Amateur - The Story of the Amateur Golf Championship 1885-1995* (Grant Books, Worchestershire, 1995)

Boswell, Thomas; *Strokes of Genius* (Doubleday & Company, Inc., New York, 1987)

Browning, Robert; *A History of Golf -The Royal and Ancient Game* (J.M. Dent, London, 1955)

Burnet, Bobby; *The St. Andrews Opens* (John Donald Publishers Ltd, Edinburgh, 1990)

Campbell, Malcolm; *The Scottish Golf Book* (Lomond Books, Edinburgh, 1999)

Clark, R.; *Golf A Royal and Ancient Game* (EP Publishing Limited, England, 1975)

Darwin, Bernard; *The Golf Courses of the British Isles* (Storey Communications/Ailsa, Inc., 1988)

Darwin, Bernard/Gardiner-Hill/ Campbell/ Cotton/ Longhurst/ Craley/ Wilson/ Lord Brabazon; *A History of Golf In Britain* (Cassell & Company Ltd, London, 1952)

Diaz, Jaime; *Hallowed Ground - Golf's Greatest Places* (The Greenwich Workshop Press, Connecticut, 1999)

Dickinson, Patric; *A Round of Golf Courses A Selection of the Best 18* (Evans Brothers Ltd, London, 1951)

Garcia, John L.B.; *Harold Hilton: His Golfing Life and Times* (Severnside Printers Limited, Baskerville, 1992)

Gibson, Nevin H.; *The Encyclopedia of Golf* (A.S. Barnes and Company, New York, 1958)

Goodner, Ross; *Golf's Greatest - The Legendary World Golf Hall of Famers* (Simon & Schuster, New York, 1978)

Grimond, Jo; *The St. Andrews of Jo Grimond* (Alan Sutton Publishing, Ltd., Gloucestershire, 1992)

Hamilton, David; *Golf Scotland's Game* (Kilmacolm, 1999)

Harris, Robert; *Sixty Years of Golf* (Batchworth Press Ltd, 1953)

Hurdzan, Dr. Michael J.; *Golf Course Architecture - Design, Construction & Restoration* (Sleeping Bear Press, Michigan, 1996)

Jackson, Alan F.; *The British Professional Golfer 1887 - 1930 A Register* (Grant Books, Worchestershire, 1994)

Johnston, Alastair J. and James F. Johnston; *The Chronicles of Golf 1457 to 1857* (1993)

Jones, Robert Tyre, Jr.; *Golf Is My Game* (Doubleday, New York, 1960)

Kirkaldy, Andra; *Fifty Years of Golf: My Memories* (USGA, New Jersey, 1993)

Lyle, Sandy with Bob Ferrier; *The Championship Courses of Scotland* (World's Work Ltd., 1982)

Macdonald, Charles Blair; *Scotland's Gift Golf* (Ailsa Inc., 1985)

MacKenzie, Alister; *The Spirit of St. Andrews* (Sleeping Bear Press, Michigan, 1995)

Mackenzie, Richard; *A Wee Nip at the 19th Hole* (Sleeping Bear Press, Michigan, 1997)

Mackie, Keith; *Golf at St. Andrews* (Aurum Press Limited, London, 1995)

McLeod, Rod; *St. Andrews Old* (Souvenir Press LTD, London, 1970)

Mortimer, Charles G. and Fred Pignon; *The Story of the Open Golf Championship 1860 to 1950* (Jarrolds Publishers, Great Britain, 1952)

Olman, Morton W. and John M.; *St. Andrews & Golf* (Market Street Press, 1995)

Olman, Morton W. and John M.; *The Encyclopedia of Golf Collectibles* (Books Americana, Inc., Alabama, 1985)

Ouimet, Francis; *A Game of Golf* (Houghton Mifflin Company, Boston and New York, 1932)

Robertson, James K.; *St. Andrews Home of Golf* (J. & G. Innes, Ltd., Scotland, 1967)

Roger, Rev. Charles; *History of St. Andrews* (Adams & Chas. Black, Edinburgh, 1849)

Salmond, J.B.; *The Story of the R&A* (MacMillan & Company LTD, London, 1956)

Sarazen, Gene; *Thirty Years of Championship Golf: The Life and Times of Gene Sarazen* (Prentice-Hall, Inc., New York, 1950)

Stanley, Louis T.; *St. Andrews* (W.H. Allen & Co. Plc, London, 1986)

Stewart, John W.; *Roland - A Short Story About Roland R. MacKenzie's Golfing Career* (Printing Corporation of America, 1987)

Taylor, Dawson; *St. Andrews Cradle of Golf* (A.S. Barnes & Co., Inc., New Jersey, 1976)

Tulloch, W.W.; *The Life of Tom Morris with Glimpses of St. Andrews and Its Golfing Celebrities* (Ellesborough Press Ltd., London, 1982)

Ward, Andrew; *Golf's Strangest Rounds* (Robson Books Ltd, London, 1992)

Ward-Thomas, Pat; *The Royal and Ancient* (Scottish Academic Press, Edinburgh, 1980)

Ward-Thomas, Pat; *The World Atlas of Golf - The Great Courses and How They Are Played* (Michael Beasley Publishers Ltd., London)

Williams, Michael; *St. Andrews Is Still The Mecca* (World of Golf, London 1982)

Wind, Herbert Warren; *Following Through* (Ticknor & Fields, New York, 1985)

Young, Douglas; *St. Andrews Town & Gown, Royal & Ancient* (Cassell & Company LTD, London, 1969)

PHOTO CREDITS

Francis Ouimet

My Personal Wry? Story
on the Road Hole

**D&W. AUCHTERLONIE
TIMBER DRYING SHEDS
SHOP 4 PILMOUR LINKS ·
WORKSHOP 9 UNION ST**

The black sheds are behind Bob Jones